Compiled by
Restaurant Recipes

*You can now prepare and taste some of your
favorite restaurant foods in your own kitchen.
Featuring over 150 Restaurant Recipes from
some of Kansas City's best known eating
and drinking establishments. Enjoy!*

D1064022

Special Thanks from the Editor:
This cookbook would not have been possible without the support of all the restaurant owners, managers, chefs and sponsors who appear in this book.

Copyright © 2005 Restaurant Recipes of Kansas City
Library of Congress Control Number: 2005904587
ISBN: 1-5859733-5-1
Second Edition

Copyright © 2006 Restaurant Recipes of Kansas City
Library of Congress Control Number: 2005904587
ISBN: 0-9778057-3-5
Special Edition (Hardcover)

Printed in China

Published by:

Restaurant Recipes
A division of JEC Publishing Co.
305 E. Walnut Street, Suite 222
Springfield, Missouri 65806
(800) 313-5121

Editor: JE Cornwell
Senior Advisor: Judith A. Cornwell
Graphic Design: Tom Dease
Project Advisor: Jim Martin

Contents

The Best of Kansas City

RESTAURANT
Recipes of
APPETIZERS

BO LINGS

Plaza Board of Trade
48th & Main • (816) 753-1718

Orchard Corner Center
95th & Quivira • (913) 888-6618

Gateway Plaza
91st & Metcalf • (913) 341-1718

Overland Park
135th & Metcalf • (913) 239-8188

www.bolings.com

Owners Richard and Theresa Ng do extensive research to ensure that all items on the menu, even the rice (a blend of aromatic jasmine long grain rice and fluffy American long grain rice), is the best available. "It is our goal to provide good, healthy food with the best service, so there is plenty of time to enjoy your meal, and sit and talk and drink tea with friends. It's part of the Chinese tradition," says Richard Ng. Local publications have named Bo Lings best Chinese restaurant in Kansas City time and again. Recently, Bo Lings was named one of the top 100 Chinese restaurants in America by national publication Chinese Restaurant News!

Shanghai Wontons

1 lb. ea. Shrimp and Pork
1 Tsp. Chopped Fresh Ginger
Dash of Sugar
1 Pkg. Thin Wonton Wrappers

1 lb. Baby Bok Choy
Salt and White Pepper to Season
2 Tsp. Sesame Seed Oil
Vegetable Oil

Directions

Chop the pork and shrimp into small pieces, and mix in seasonings and sesame seed oil. Blanche Bok Choy, and squeeze water out of Bok Choy. Then chop up Bok Choy and mix with pork/shrimp mixture. Wrap a big teaspoonful in each wrapper; then pan fry or deep fry in vegetable oil, or boil wontons in water.

Submitted by Bo Lings Fine Chinese Cuisine

Don Ruby's Taqueria

33495 Lexington Ave.
DeSoto, Kansas
(913) 585-1940
Fax (913) 585-1805

Owner Ruben Campos, is a native of Zacatecas, Mexico, but he immigrated to the United States in 1993. He and wife Norma own Chelly's Cafe together before deciding they would branch out to DeSoto.

Don Ruby's serves only the most authentic Mexican cuisine. It's made fresh daily, nothing is reheated. They will offer nearly one full page of drink specials, including many imported liquors. The cantina boasts a breakfast menu, lunch specials and dinner combos, all at a very affordable prices. The beverage list includes horchata and the dessert list boasts delicious sopapillas.

Don Ruby's Taqueria is worth the drive on Kansas Hwy. 10 to DeSoto. Enjoy Ruben's tamales and chicken enchiladas with a cold beverage.

Coctel de Camarón (Shrimp Coctel)

12 Med. Shrimp, Cooked & Deveined
1 Med. Onion, Chopped
1/2 Avacado, Diced
2 Tbs. Fresh Lime Juice

2 Diced Tomatoes
1 Jalapeno Pepper, Sliced
1 Tbs. Cilantro
Salt & Pepper to Taste

Directions

Mix all ingredients together. Serve chilled with wedge of lemon or lime.

Submitted by Ruben Campos

HEREFORD HOUSE

★★★★ KANSAS CITY'S ORIGINAL ★★★★

20th & Main, Kansas City, MO • (816) 842-1080
5001 Town Center Drive, Leawood, KS • (913) 327-0800
4931 W. 6th Street, Lawrence, KS • (785) 842-2333
19721 E. Jackson Dr., Independence, MO • (816) 795-9200
Zona Rosa – 8661 Stoddard, North Kansas City, MO 64153 • (816) 584-9000

Very few American steakhouses come close to the consistent excellence and quality standards that The Hereford House has mastered for nearly 48 years. Even fewer have earned the national reputation that makes this independent restaurant a favorite of legendary sports figures, Hollywood celebrities and even a few U.S. Presidents.

What's our secret? Sterling Silver Premium Beef. It comes from premium cattle bred and raised in the high plains of North America. We like to say that Hereford House beef makes life taste better.

With five locations around the metro area, you'll never find yourself too far away from this Kansas City tradition. Go ahead. Consider tonight's dinner plans made. Fire up your car and head over to one of our area restaurants. We'll fire up our grill for the best steak dinner you've ever enjoyed. See you at the Hereford House!

Seafood Stuffed Mushrooms

1-1/2 lbs. Cream Cheese (softened)	3 Egg Yolks
1/4 Cup Italian Bread Crumbs	3 Green Onions (chopped)
Lemon Juice (fresh squeezed) 1 lemon	Splash Worcestershire Sauce
1/2 Tbsp. Garlic Powder	1/2 Tbsp. Salt
Pinch White Pepper	1/2 lb. Snow Crab (thawed)
1/2 lb. Bay Shrimp (thawed)	1/2 lb. Flake Crab Meat (thawed)

Directions

Place cream cheese into bowl of Kitchen-Aid along with egg yolks, bread crumbs, green onions, lemon juice, and Worcestershire sauce. With paddle attachment, turn the mixer on low. Increase speed as cheese softens. In a separate container, mix seasonings together and add to the cheese mixture. Continue mixing to blend ingredients well.

Take seafood and squeeze to remove excess water. Place seafood into mixture with cheese and mix on low speed until just incorporated.

De-stem large mushrooms and place on cookie sheet and bake for about 10 minutes. Cool. With a kitchen spoon, fill mushroom caps with seafood filling. Roll stuffed caps in Italian bread crumbs. Bake at 400 degrees for about 10 minutes or until browned. Filling can also be used to stuff chicken, as a steak topper, stuffing for fish, or thinned out and used as a pasta sauce.

Submitted by Hereford House

JESS & JIM'S STEAKHOUSE

JESS & JIM'S STEAKHOUSE
FAMILY OWNED AND OPERATED
SINCE 1938

135th & Locust
Kansas City, MO (Martin City)
(816) 941-9499
Lunch: Mon-Sat 11 a.m. - 3 p.m.
Dinner: Mon-Thur 3 p.m. - 10 p.m.
Fri-Sat 3 p.m. - 10 p.m.
Sunday 12 p.m. - 9 p.m.

Jess and Jim's Steak House opened for business in April, 1938, by two men who were best friends. Jess Kincaid and Jim Wright started their business at 135th & Holmes as a small bar and grill, relocating to their present location after a tornado in 1957.

Jess and Jim believed that good food, good service and fair prices would make the drive far south of the city worthwhile. This became what is known today as Jess & Jim's Steak House.

Jess left the business after starting a family, leaving Jim to run it. Jim hired his cousin, R.C. VanNoy to host and manage the dining room at night. This worked well with Jim in the kitchen and R.C. in the dining room.

An article in a 1972 issue of Playboy magazine written by Calvin Trillin, brought Jess & Jim's Steak House national fame. So much so, we named a steak after it.

Jim's health started failing in 1977 and he left R.C. to run things. Jess & Jim have since passed. R.C. also passed in October of 2002. Mike and David (his sons) have owned the restaurant since 1990. Now the 4th generation is working and grooming to take over the business someday. Jess & Jim's Steak House, since 1938, has been a family owned and operated restaurant.

Jess & Jim's Steak House Shrimp Scampi

4 oz. Butter
1/4 Cup lemon juice, fresh & squeezed
1 tsp. Tabasco sauce
1 Cup bread crumbs

1 clove garlic, peeled & smashed
2 Cups white wine
1 Cup shallots, chopped
20 large shrimp, peeled & deveined

Directions

In a sauté pan, over low heat, combine butter, garlic, lemon juice, white wine and Tabasco. Add shallots & bread crumbs to mixture. Blend well. Add shrimp and stir occasionally to coat shrimp. Allow the shrimp to cook until they are plump and firm, approximately 12 minutes.

Submitted by the VanNoy Family

MARGARITA'S AUTHENTIC MEXICAN FOOD

Margarita's Authentic Mexican Food

7013 N. Oak
Gladstone, MO
(816) 468-0337

12200 Johnson Dr.
Shawnee, KS
(913) 631-5553

2829 Southwest Blvd.
Kansas City, MO
(816) 931-4849

13401 Holmes
Kansas City, MO
(816) 941-9411

There are many aspects to Margarita's success. One is their philosophy that "the customer is number one." There is something to please everyone on their extensive menu. Another is old family recipes that help Chef John Abarca to dish up authentic Mexican food that melts in your mouth and keeps customers loyal and coming back. They pride themselves on using the best products and ingredients they can buy. Let's not forget where Margarita's got its name. It is named for the popular Mexican drink that contains tequila, triple sec and other ingredients. At the restaurant Margarita's are made in large batches then dispensed through a tap like draught beef. When you go to Margarita's you know you will get good service, drinks, and most importantly good food, in short it feels like coming home.

Margarita's Chorizo Rumaki

1/2 lb. Chorizo Sausage, Removed from the Casing, Cooked
40 ea. Dates, Sliced Down One Side and Opened
20 ea. Bacon Slices Cut in Half
2 Cups Soy Sauce
1/2 Cup Brown Sugar
1/2 Cup Whole Grain Mustard
1/2 Cup Honey

Directions

Fill each date with 1/2 tsp. of chorizo. Wrap each filled date with 1/2 slice of bacon and secure with a toothpick.

Combine the soy sauce and the brown sugar. Marinate the bacon wrapped dates for 1-1/2 hours. Remove from marinade and bake on a parchment paper lined sheet pan 15 minutes or until the bacon is crisp. Mix honey and whole grain mustard for the dipping sauce.

Submitted by David and Ron

PIROPOS RESTAURANT

PIROPOS
RESTAURANT

A Taste of Argentina
ON THE HILL
DOWNTOWN PARKVILLE

I West First Street
Parkville, MO 64152
(816) 741-3600
Fax (816) 741-3615
www.piroposkc.com

The taste of Argentina is very American Midwestern. The foods of its capital city Buenos Aires, are steaks, grilled meats, seafood, fresh salads and vegetables. Argentinean dining is very cosmopolitan with a touch of Spanish, Italian, French and other ethnic foods. The food is simple, not particularly spicy, yet flavorful. Piropos imports all of its salts, butter, cheese and spice from Argentina. Strongly European in background and culture, Argentineans enjoy dining in a generally relaxed atmosphere where conversation and gracious dining go hand-in-hand. Overlooking quaint downtown Parkville and Park University makes one feel as though they are dining in a small European Village. Piropos Restaurant, on the hill in downtown Parkville, offers a unique view, warm atmosphere and fresh foods prepared in the Argentinean style.

Lobster Cakes

1 cup Red bell pepper, diced
1 cup corn
2 tablespoons, lemon juice
1 bunch parsley, chopped
1 cup plain bread crumbs

1 cup Green bell pepper, diced
1 cup Lobster meat, cooked
1 cup mayonnaise
2 eggs
1 teaspoon salt and pepper, each

Directions

Mix all the ingredients, except for the lobster meat, together. Carefully fold in the lobster meat so as not to break up the pieces too much. Divide into 2 1/2 ounce cakes. Coat in plain bread crumbs. Place 1 tbsp. oil in frying pan. Cook 1 minute on each side and finish in oven at 350 degrees for 3 minutes.

Submitted by Piropos Restaurant

RJ'S BOB-BE-QUE SHACK

5835 Lamar
Mission, KS 66202
(913) 262-7300
Fax (913) 262-7323

Executive Chef Robert M. Palmgren (Bob) fulfilled his life long dream on Oct. 31, 2003 when he opened the doors to this new restaurant, RJ's Bob-Be-Que Shack.

At the age of 13 Bob got his first taste of the food business by working in the family grocery store. In 1982 he entered his first American Royal BBQ contest. Since then he was competed in over 100 contests and received numerous awards. BBQ tradition is to put your name on your product. To accomplish this Bob has worked hard for 20 years on improving and perfecting his product.

In trying to keep the family tradition going, RJ's is named after Bob's son, Robert Jr. Also, "Angie's tossed salad" on his menu is named after his daughter Angela. "Bob-Be-Que" is his team competition name.

RJ's Jalapeno Sausages in Corn Husk

5 lbs. Pork Butte, Coarse Grinds
1/2 oz. Sugar
2 Tsp. Garlic, Fresh, Chopped
1/2 Tsp. Allspice
2 T. Crushed Black Peppercorns
Dry Corn Husk

1.2 oz. Kosher Salt
1 oz. Chicken Base
1 Tsp. Nutmeg
1/2 Cup Jalapenos, Seeded, Chopped Medium
1 Tsp. Cayenne Pepper

Directions

Have your butcher grind the pork butte for you if you do not have a grinder attachment. Soak corn husk in warm water for 15 minutes. Prepare and measure all ingredients before making the sausage. Combine all ingredients in a Kitchen aide mixer with the paddle attachment. Mix only until all ingredients are incorporated. Don't over mix. Scoop out approximately 3 oz. of sausage and place in open corn husk. Tie each end with string.

Smoke at 250 Degrees F. for approximately 2 hours or until internal temperature reaches 160 degrees F. Serve with RJ's Hot BBQ Sauce and Dijon Mustard as an appetizer or slice and make sandwiches. Yields 25 sausages.

Enjoy with your favorite beverage!

Submitted by Executive Chef Robert M. Palmgren

SPECTATORS SPORTS BAR

CROWN CENTER RESTAURANTS BY HYATT
Spectators Sports Bar
2345 McGee Street
Kansas City, MO 64108
(816) 435-4199, Fax (816) 421-1550

Spectators Sports Bar is located on the mezzanine level of Hyatt Regency Crown Center and is the perfect place to come, relax, eat and watch your favorite teams. From the Starting Line-up to the Main Event and Even into Extra Innings, Spectators has your taste buds covered. With a big screen TV, the ESPN game Plan, a pool table, and arcade games, Spectators is the place to be if you are a fan of any game.

Buffalo Wings

Chicken Wings (Bone In/Bone Out) 2 packages

Sauce:
16 oz. Franks Hot Sauce
1 lb. Melted Butter
1-1/2 Tbsp. Garlic Powder
Vegetable Oil (optional)
Celery Sticks (optional)

1 cup Honey (warm)
1 Tbsp. Cayenne Pepper (to taste)
1-1/2 Tbsp. Onion Powder
Blue Cheese/Ranch Dressing (optional)

Directions

Preheat oven to 375 degrees. Add together melted butter, cayenne pepper, garlic powder and onion powder and mix well. Then add warm honey and Frank's hot sauce to hot sauce mixture. Place chicken wings on baking sheet. (To keep from sticking, lightly coat with vegetable oil.) When oven is ready, place baking sheet with wings in the oven for 20-30 minutes. When finished, toss chicken wings in hot sauce mixture and enjoy wings with cool Blue Cheese/Ranch Dressing.

Submitted by Cathy Novak, Sous Chef

TERRACE ATRIUM RESTAURANT

CROWN CENTER RESTAURANTS BY HYATT
Terrace Atrium Restaurant
2345 McGee Street
Kansas City, MO 64108
(816) 435-4199, Fax (816) 421-1550

The Terrace Restaurant, located on the mezzanine level of Hyatt Regency Crown Center is the perfect place to relax while enjoying your meal. The beautiful garden setting surrounded by lush greenery and tranquil waters is sure to satisfy your need to unwind. The Terrace offers both a daily breakfast buffet and salad deli-bar as well as a variety of tasty menu selections. For an express breakfast, visit Coffee Express at the entrance of the Terrace for specialty coffees, danish, and more.

Chicken Nachos

6 oz. Red, yellow and blue corn tortilla chips
2 oz. Pizza cheese
2 oz. Diced tomatoes
1 oz.Sliced black olives
2 oz. Salsa

6 oz. Grated cheddar cheese
3 oz. Grilled chicken, diced
2 oz. Sliced jalapenos
2 oz. Sour cream

Directions

Spread chips evenly over entire surface or pasta bowl. Top with 3 oz. of cheddar cheese and 1 oz. of pizza cheese. Add tomatoes, jalapenos, black olives, and grilled chicken. Top with remaining cheese and cook in a 400 degree oven for 1-1/2 minutes. Serve with salsa and sour cream on the side.

Submitted by Cathy Novak, Sous Chef

THE CAPITAL GRILLE

On The Country Club Plaza
4740 Jefferson Street
Kansas City, MO 64112
(816) 531-8345
We offer private dining for 8 to 80 at lunch or dinner.

The Capital Grille located on the Country Club Plaza is home of our dry aged, hand cut Kansas City Strip, the freshest Seafood and mouth watering Chops. Come see why one Ingram's critic wrote, "I was speechless." Yet Ingram's was not speechless about our service... which was voted best in Kansas City in 2004. For a really special night join us for the lively and sophisticated sounds of our Sunday night Jazz. Find out why nothing says "Kansas City" more than cutting into a perfectly prepared, dry aged steak and listening to the beautiful, soulful sounds of live music in the background. For special celebrations or the business meeting that has to be just right, trust our professional service staff under the guidance of Executive Chef, Ray Comiskey and his culinary team to wow you every time. Whenever you think of The Capital Grille, think of a perfectly crafted, unforgettable meal, whether it is a under-an-hour power lunch or a private dinner event in one of our five spectacular private dining rooms.

Pan Roasted Lobster

Lobster Meat: 2 appetizer portions or 1 dinner portion

10 oz Lobster Meat, cooked and shelled (2 tails, 2 claws, 2 knuckles

6 Tbsp Unsalted Whole Butter	1/2 Tbsp Freshly Chopped Tarragon
1/2 Tbsp Freshly Chopped Chives	1/2 Tbsp Freshly Chopped Chervil
1 tsp Kosher Sale	6 oz Seasonal Vegetable Garnish

1/4 oz Micro Green or Sprouts

1. Melt 2 Tbsp. of whole butter in a sauté pan over medium heat. 2. Once the butter is melted, add the lobster to the pan and cook for one minute, being careful not to brown. 3. Add the seasonal vegetable garnish and an additional 2 Tbsp. of butter, gently stirring to combine and evenly heat. 4. Reduce the heat to low, add the last 2 Tbsp. of butter, the fresh herbs, and season with the kosher salt. 5. Carefully separate the seasonal garnish from the lobster with a spoon and place in the center of two warmed bowls. 6. Place 1 claw, 1 knuckle, and 1 tail over the vegetable garnish and drizzle butter pan sauce over and around the lobster. 7. Place a silver dollar-sized bunch of micro greens on top of the lobster and serve immediately.

Vegetable Garnish: 2 orders (12 oz.)

4 oz Asparagus (sliced on extreme bias)	2 ears or 4 oz Freshly Shucked Corn, cut off cob
4 oz Oyster Mushrooms, sliced thinly	2 oz Unsalted Whole Butter
1/2 gal Water	1 tsp Kosher Salt
1 Tbsp Sugar	

1. Combine the water, salt and sugar, and bring to a boil. 2. Add the corn and cook for four minutes. 3. While the corn is cooking, add the butter to a large sauté pan and warm over medium heat. 4. Add the mushrooms and cook, stirring frequently, for three minutes. Season with 1 tsp. of salt and place the mushrooms in a mixing bowl. 5. Add the sliced asparagus to the blanching water and cook with the corn for one minute. Drain the vegetables and mix them with the mushrooms. Spread out on cookie sheet and reserve for time of service.

To make this a complete meal, you can serve the pan-roasted lobster and vegetables over angel hair pasta.

Submitted by Executive Chef Ray Comiskey

COPA ROOM

3421 Broadway
Kansas City, Missouri 64111
(816) 931-5200
www.coparoomkc.com

We opened in April 2004. It did not take long and the rave reviews starting coming in from the local critics and newspapers. The original Rat Pack may be gone, but their presence is alive in this small, family run Italian restaurant. You will find fabulous food, great service and divine entertainment in this place we call home. Owner, Carlo Cammisano, could not have been blessed with a better chef than his own mother, Kathy Fiorello. When she agreed to be the chef he know he had the key ingredient for success.

Copa Room Frozia
(Italian style omelet appetizer)

4 eggs
1/2 Cup Imported Romano Cheese (grated)
1 Heaping tbsp. Fresh Chopped Sweet Basil
Pinch of Pepper
3 tbsp. Pure Olive Oil

1/2 Cup Heavy Whipping Cream
1 Heaping tbsp. Fresh Chopped Garlic
Pinch of Salt
1 Cup Chopped Raw Vegetable of your
  choice (asparagus, broccoli, peas,
  mushrooms, artichokes)

Directions

The first step is to get a 6-in. non-stick skillet. Add 2 tbsp. of Pure Olive Oil. Add raw vegetables. Sauté on low to medium heat. While vegetables are being sautéd combine all other ingredients in a large bowl. Whisk until fluffy. Once the vegetables are sautéd, pour fluffy mixture over veggies. Run a spatula along the edge of the skillet until the bottom of the egg mixture sets. Once the mixture is set, take a flat plate, put on top of the skillet. Flip frozia over onto the plate, and then slide the uncooked side back into the skillet. Put in the oven at 400 degrees for 5 to 10 minutes (or until done). To make sure it is done, cut into the middle with a knife to check. Sprinkle fresh Romano cheese and fresh sweet basil on top. Cut into your choice of serving slices.

Submitted by Head Chef, Kathy Fiorello
Carlo Cammisano, Owner

TOMFOOLERIES RESTAURANT & BAR

ON THE PLAZA
612 W. 47th St.
(816) 753-0555

NORTH KC (ZONA ROSA)
8680 NW Prairie View Rd.
(816) 746-8668

tomfooleries.com

Tomfooleries...cause you had so much fun last time! A fun, come as you are atmosphere serving the local Kansas City crowd for over 14 years. Accommodations for both small and large parties looking for a variety of innovative and unique menu options.

Shrimp and Vegetable Spring Rolls with Soy Ginger Dipping Sauce

Ingredients-Spring Roll

2 oz. dried mai fun noodles (thin rice stick noodles)

12 oz. cooked shrimp

1 cup finely chopped red cabbage

1/2 cup finely chopped green onions

1/4 cup finely chopped red pepper

1 teaspoon rice wine vinegar

16 rice paper wrappers

1 cup finely chopped green cabbage

1/2 cup finely peeled carrot

1/2 cup chopped bean sprouts

2 teaspoons teriyaki sauce

2 Tablespoons finely chopped cilantro

1 large egg, beaten to blend

Ingredients-Soy Ginger Dipping Sauce

1/2 cup soy sauce

1/4 cup rice wine vinegar

4 teaspoons minced ginger

1/4 cup corn syrup

2 green onions finely chopped

1 splash of hot chili sauce

Directions

Cook noodles in pot of boiling water until tender, about 1 minute. Drain well. Coarsely chop. Place noodles in mixing bowl toss with remaining ingredients. Salt and pepper to taste. Place 1 piece rice paper on work surface. Place a 1/4 cup of mixture along center of wrapper. Fold the bottom of wrapper over filling, then fold in sides of wrapper over filling. Brush top edge of wrapper with egg. Roll up tightly, pressing to seal edge. Repeat with remaining wrappers and shrimp mixture. Cover, chill.

For Soy-Ginger Sauce- Whisk all ingredients to blend.

Submitted by Tomfooleries

V's Italian Ristorante

RISTORANTE

For over 40 years...

"A nice place to fall in love"

10819 E. 40 Hwy., Independence, MO
(816) 353-1242
11 a.m. - 9:30 p.m. M-Th.
11 a.m. - 10:30 p.m. Fri.
11:30 a.m. - 10:30 p.m. Sat.
10 a.m. - 8 p.m. Sunday
All major credit cards.
Reservations always accepted.
(816) 353-1241
www.VsRestaurant.com

Long known as Kansas City's "premier" Italian Restaurant, this family owned and operated establishment has been an important part of the city's dining experience for over 40 years.

V's formula for pleasing its guests is simply combining uncompromised service in a beautiful, relaxed environment. We offer a wide variety of authentic Italian specialties at moderate prices. Whether a romantic dinner for two, elegant formal dinner party, birthday or anniversary celebration; you'll understand why V's Italiano has become known as "a nice place to fall in love."

In addition V's also features the "Best Sunday Brunch in Town," award winning menus & wine lists and complete banquet of of-premise catering facilities. V's Italiano is the area's "must see" Italian restaurant. Located 2 miles east of the Truman Sports Complex on Highway 40

Chicken Pesto Pizza

1 8" focaccia bread   2 oz. Pesto Sauce
4 oz. grilled chicken breast (diced or cut in strips)
1 oz. diced red onion   1 oz. shredded mozzarella cheese
1 oz. grated Romano cheese

Directions

Spread pesto onto facaccia bread, top with chicken, onion, mozzarella and romano. Bake 5-8 minutes at 450 degrees, until cheese has slightly browned. Cut into fourths. Serves 1 or 2 if served with a nice salad.

Submitted by Greg Hunsucker

RESTAURANT

Recipes of

SOUPS & SALADS

75TH STREET BREWERY

520 W. 75th Street
Kansas City, MO 64114
(816) 520-4677
Fax (816) 822-2578

3512 Clinton Parkway
Lawrence, KS 66047
(785) 856-2337
Fax (785) 856-2313

Kansas City's first brewpub is still going strong now with a 2nd location in Lawrence. Check out the fresh award-winning beers in many styles. As always the made from scratch menu has something for everyone. The atmosphere is warm and inviting with TVs and live entertainment. Check us out!

Baked Potato Soup

1 Baked potato (cubed)
1 Chopped yellow onion
Tsp. Black pepper
4 oz. Butter
1 T. Chicken Base
1 Pt. Heavy cream
1 T. Kosher salt

4 oz. Chopped bacon (raw)
1 Chopped carrot
3 Ribs of chopped celery
4 oz. Flour
1 Qt. Water
1 Tsp. Tabasco sauce

Directions

Sauté all vegetables with bacon with butter in a large skillet over medium heat.

When bacon and vegetables are cooked add flour and stir occasionally. Continue cooking for 5 minutes

Add the rest of the ingredients and bring to a simmer. Simmer for 15 -20 minutes. Garnish with fresh chopped scallions.

Submitted by KC Hopps, Ltd.

AMERISPORTS BREW PUB

AMERISTAR CASINO & HOTEL
Amerisports Brew Pub
3200 North Ameristar Drive
Kansas City, MO 64161
(800) 499-4961 or (816) 414-7000

This $6 million sports bar and brew pub features a state-of-the art video system, the only German-style lager house in the area, and a hearty menu offering lunch, dinner and late-night dining. The comfortable 135-seat sports bar offers guests such classics as giant pretzels, Buffalo wings and heaping macho nachos. Other selections include an array of juicy burgers, sandwiches, crisp salads, smokehouse pulled pork, baby back ribs and sizzling fajitas. Amerisports also offers five custom-brewed German-style lagers including the "Knock Out Blond" (Pilsner), "Red Zone" (Munchner), "Half Court" (Helles), "Hard Ball" (Dunkel), and a rotating "Draft Choice Special" brew will fill out the offerings

Amerisports Blackened Salmon Salad

Serves 1

4 oz. Iceberg Lettuce
7 oz. Salmon Fillet
4 oz. Roasted Corn
1 ea. Tomato Quartered
2 Tbsp. Seasoned Flour

2 oz. Spring Mix
1 oz. Blackening Spice
4 oz. Dressing
2 oz. Sliced Onions

Directions

Toss onions in flour and deep fry crisp, reserve. Season salmon with blackening spice and sear at high heat until done. Toss lettuce with corn and dressing of choice. Arrange on plate and place salmon on top of green. Garnish with fried onions and tomatoes.

We serve this salad on a grilled flat bread.

Submitted by Edward Allen, Executive Chef

B.B.'S LAWNSIDE BAR-B-Q

1205 E. 85th Street
Kansas City, MO 64131
(816) 8BB-RIBS (822-7427)
www.bbslawnsidebbq.com

Kitchen Hours:
Wed. 11 a.m. - 10 p.m.
Thurs. 11 a.m. - 10:30 p.m.
Fri. & Sat. 11 a.m. - 11 p.m.
Sunday 4 p.m. - 10:30 p.m.

Where Bar-B-Q Meets the Blues

For a full shot of what Kansas City does best–blues and barbecue–you can't beat Lindsay and Jo Shannon's roadhouse. The tradition of bar-b-q and blues in Kansas City had its start in the 1930's when Count Basie, Joe Turner and Charlie Parker hung out at the Old Kentucky Bar-B-Q near 18th and Vine. The granite stones that were used to build B.B.'s bbq pit in 1950 came from the gravel streets downtown where they served as crosswalks...Perhaps Joe Turner once high stepped across these same granite stones.

The granite stones hold heat, allowing a slow-smoke cooking process. Briskets are smoked 14-16 hours and ribs 10-12 hours, using an indirect heat source fueled by hickory wood. All meats on our menu, including sausage and chicken, are slow-smoked on the over 50-year-old pit. When the blues music floats off the bandstand, it wafts across your plate of bbq, imparting a flavor you can only get in Kansas City at B.B.'s Lawnside Bar-B-Q.

Burnt End Soup

2 Medium Size Burnt Ends
1 Bag Carrots
1 Large Yellow Onion
2 Large Cans Beef Broth (2) 49 oz.
1 Small Can Diced Tomatoes 14.5 oz.
1/2 Tsp. Mild Red Pepper
1 Tbsp. Black Pepper

2 Whole Potatoes
1 Small to Medium Bunch Celery
4 Tbsp. Worcestershire Sauce
1/2 Large Can Water
2 Tbsp. Garlic Powder
1 Tsp. Salt

Directions

Peel vegetables and sauté in half stick butter. Add all other ingredients except burnt ends. Bring to a boil and continue boiling for approx. 15 minutes. Reduce heat and add burnt ends. Simmer for another 20 minutes. (Burnt ends should be cut into small pieces.)

Submitted by Lindsay Shannon

BO LINGS

Plaza Board of Trade
48th & Main • (816) 753-1718

Orchard Corner Center
95th & Quivira • (913) 888-6618

Gateway Plaza
91st & Metcalf • (913) 341-1718

Overland Park
135th & Metcalf • (913) 239-8188

www.bolings.com

Owners Richard and Theresa Ng do extensive research to ensure that all items on the menu, even the rice (a blend of aromatic jasmine long grain rice and fluffy American long grain rice), is the best available. "It is our goal to provide good, healthy food with the best service, so there is plenty of time to enjoy your meal, and sit and talk and drink tea with friends. It's part of the Chinese tradition," says Richard Ng. Local publications have named Bo Lings best Chinese restaurant in Kansas City time and again. Recently, Bo Lings was named one of the top 100 Chinese restaurants in America by national publication Chinese Restaurant News!

Bo Lings Long Life Noodle Soup

Rice Noodles – 4 6-oz. dry; soak in cool water   Stock
One Whole Chicken (Remove all skin, and chop up breast meat.
Rinse the rest of chicken.
Boil 4 qts. water. When boiling, add chicken, bring water to boil. Keep in high heat for 5 minutes, remove top layer of oil.

1 Clove Garlic, Peel, Chop	Chicken Breast Meat, Cut in Strips
3 oz. Medium Shrimp, Peel and de-vein ter,	2 oz. Fresh Spinach, Soak in Cold Wa-
2 Eggs Pan-Fried, Set Aside	Drain, Then Chop Into Smaller Pieces
1 Tbsp. Cooking Oil	1 Tsp. Sesame Seed Oil
2 Tbsp. Soy Sauce	Pinch of Salt and White Pepper

Directions

To cook noodles:

Boil 3 qt. of water, when boiling, remove rice noodles from cold water, add to hot water, boil for three minutes, drain, rinse with cold water and set aside.

In sauce pan or wok, heat to smoking, add cooking oil, garlic, chicken meat, stir. When meat turns white, add shrimp, and stir until just turn pink. Add 5 cups of stock, seasoning, and spinach. Turn off heat.

In 2 large bowls, put rice noodles on bottom, ladle soup just finished, top with fried egg. Serves 2.

Submitted by Bo Lings Fine Chinese Cuisine

6001 Johnson Drive
Mission, KS 66205
(913) 671-8199
Fax (913) 671-8715

Monday-Saturday
7 a.m. - 3 p.m.

Chacko's began as a catering company in our home in 1998. We quickly gained a following with our lunch boxes and had to move to our current location. We wanted to use the knowledge of breakfast pastries that David learned while attending California Culinary Academy. Chacko's Bakery and Catering opened in May of 2000.

Chacko's is named after our 9 year old son. Elizabeth, our 11 year-old daughter, has our corner store and breads named after her.

We offer a small dine in area and have opened the "Corner Store" which offers many of our new creations for you to take home and enjoy, including soups, stocks, dips, dressings and take home meals.

We are located on Johnson Drive. Two blocks east of Lamar and one block west of Woodson on the south side of the street. Look for our green awning.

We look forward to you becoming one of our "Roll Models," or a "Chackoholic."

Mixed Green Salad with Dried Apricots, Goat Cheese and Honey Lemon Vinaigrette

1 lb. Spring Mix Lettuce or Field Greens
1/4 Cup Honey (clover or wildflower)
4 oz. Goat Cheese
1/4 Cup Honey Lemon Vinaigrette (see recipe)

1 Cup Dried Apricots, Chopped
1/4 Cup Hot Water
1/4 Cup Toasted Sunflower Seeds (unsalted)

Directions

In a small bowl combine honey and hot water and dissolve honey. Add the apricots and allow to set aside for 10-15 minutes, drain. Divide mixed greens among individual plates or in a large bowl and top with goat cheese, apricots and sunflower seeds. Drizzle with vinaigrette and enjoy.

Honey Lemon Vinaigrette

1/4 Cup Fresh Lemon Juice
1/2 Cup Clover Honey
1/2 Tsp. Fresh Black Pepper

3/4 Cup Canola Oil
1/2 Tsp. Salt

Directions

Whisk vinaigrette ingredients together. Chill until ready to serve. May be made up to 1 week in advance. Yields 1-1/2 cups.

Submitted by Rachel and David Finn

CRAYOLA CAFÉ

CROWN CENTER RESTAURANTS BY HYATT
Crayola Café
2450 Grand Street
Kansas City, MO 64108
(816) 435-4128, Fax (816) 435-4136

Crayola Café adds a fun and colorful atmosphere to any dining experience! Sporting bright, colorful décor and placemats that serve as blank canvasses, Crayola Café is the perfect place to revisit your childhood and explore your inner artist.

The menu at Crayola Café features a blend of traditional favorites and creative originals sure to please even the toughest critic. Don't forget, Crayola Café also has a party room that is the perfect place to celebrate a birthday or any special occasion.

Crayola Salad

3 oz. Spring Mix
1 oz. Orange Segments
1.5 oz. Feta Cheese

2 oz. Strawberries
1 oz. Sugar Glazed Walnuts (will need to prepare)
2 oz. Poppy Seed Dressing

Sugar Glazed Walnuts:
4 oz. Walnuts
4 tbls. Egg Whites
1 tsp. Cinnamon

Directions

For the Walnuts: Whip egg whites with sugar and cinnamon until they form soft peaks. Toss walnuts in egg white mixture and place on a sheet tray and bake until golden brown.

Place spring mix into a bowl. Add all of the ingredients and toss with your favorite.

Submitted by Dominic Vaccaro, Executive Sous Chef, CCRH

DAN'S LONGBRANCH STEAKHOUSE

Dan's LONGBRANCH STEAKHOUSE

9095 Metcalf
Overland Park, KS
(913) 642-9555

Our recipes are made from scratch, from our homemade salad dressings to our monster twice-baked potato. We char-grill our fresh steaks, burgers and chicken breasts to your specifications and hand-batter our chicken-fried steaks and chicken breast.

We assure you a delicious, complete meal to make your hectic days easier!

Just pick up the phone and we will deliver direct to you a full-course great meal at a great price with great taste...FROM OUR STEAKHOUSE TO YOUR HOUSE!

Dan's Steak Soup

1 Onion - Medium Diced
2 Ribs Celery - Chopped
2 lbs. Cubed Beef
1 Cup Mushrooms - Medium Chopped
1 Tsp. Tabasco
Salt & Black Pepper - Season to Taste

2 Cloves Garlic - Fine Diced
2 Carrots - Chopped
1 Can. Tomatoes in Juice
1 Cup Corn
1/2 Gal. Beef Broth
2 Potatoes - Cubed

Directions

Brown cubed beef. Sauté onions, add garlic, celery and carrots. Add meat and continue to brown together (10-15 minutes) Add tomatoes. Cook for about 10 minutes. Add beef broth and simmer for 5 minutes. Add remainder of ingredients and simmer for 10 more minutes. Season to taste.

Submitted by Dan Greet

DINKY & COCO'S CAFE

14383 Metcalf Ave.
Overland Park, KS 66223
(913) 897-3800

Dinky & Coco's Cafe', the idea for the business came from a love of both coffee and ice cream from the owner Gale Hammond and the enormous love for her dogs, Dinky and Coco. The store is divided strategically into two sections, one entrance brings you into the Espresso Bar that feautures gourmet brewed coffee from fresh roasted beans and an extensive menu of hot, iced, and frozen espresso beverages. Casual and comfortable seating for about 20 people on this side plus abundant outdoor seating make this a great spot for small business meetings and social get togethers.

Step over to the other side of the store and a whole new world awaits you!! You have entered "Gelato Paradise" where they make homemade Italian Ice Cream in over 100 flavors from the finest ingredients. Dinky & Coco's uses only the most choice quality products imported from Italy. Customers rave about their flavors and incredible quality. They make custom Italian Ice Cream Pies to order and make special order gelato for parties and special events of all kinds. They also make custom gift baskets for all occasions and have gift cards available for purchase.

Gale's California Western Wilted Salad

Fresh Leaf Lettuce or Spring Mix
2 hard cooked eggs
1/2 c. water
1 T. sugar
Fresh cracked pepper

2 or 3 green onions
3 sliced smoked bacon
3 T. balsamic vinegar
1 tsp. salt

Directions

Tear lettuce leaves and add green onions, chopped. Slice egg-centers reserving several slices for garnish; cut up remaining eggs and toss in. Fry bacon, remove and crumble over lettuce. Add other ingredients to bacon drippings and bring to a rapid boil. Pour over lettuce, garnish with egg slices and fresh cracked pepper and serve at once.

Submitted by Gale Hammond

DON CHILITO'S MEXICAN RESTAURANT

Don Chilito's
MEXICAN RESTAURANT

7017 Johnson Drive
Mission, KS
(913) 432-4615

Don Chilito's Mexican Restaurant is one of Kansas City's oldest and best known restaurants. It has served more than 9 million meals in 34 years. It was the forerunner of today's fast casual fresh mex operations. In fact, they are doing what we did more than 30 years ago.

Don Chilito's mission statement was to consistently serve the best Mexican food with a choice of portion sizes at the lowest possible prices with the quickest service. All recipes are original and prepared from scratch all day every day. Our order line moves very fast and there is no tipping. We are serving third generation customers and welcome your patronage. We save you time and save you money–both of which you may spend on other things. Fast service–not fast food.

Don's Spicy Gazpacho

2 Large Cucumbers
8 Ripe Tomatoes
2 Cloves Garlic, Minced
1/2 Tsp. Ground Cumin
1 Bunch Fresh Cilantro
1 Tbsp. Tobasco Sauce

2 Med. Green Bell Peppers
1 Onion, Finely Chopped
4 Tsp. Olive Oil
2 Tsp. Sherry Vinegar
3 Tbsp. Prepared Horseradish
1 46 oz. Can Tomato Juice

Directions

Peel and de-seed cucumbers, tomatoes, green peppers with the garlic, olive oil, vinegar, cilantro, horseradish and tobasco n food processor or blender. Process with approximately one-half the tomato juice to make a smooth puree.

Combine pureed soup with remaining chopped vegetables in one gallon container, salt and pepper to taste and shake vigorously.

Cooks Tip: Let chill and marinade in refrigerator for 24 hours. Serve cold with an ice cube. This soup gets better with age.

Submitted by Barry Cowden

EBT RESTAURANT

EBT

1310 Carondelet Drive
(I-435 & State Line)
Kansas City, MO
(816) 942-8870 • www.EBTrestaurant.com

EBT is a Kansas City tradition that was originally run by Myron Green Cafeteria's and is now run by Treat America Food Services, which has been nominated in One Of The Top Ten Small Businesses of Kansas City for 2005. EBT's is a full service restaurant that offers lunch and dinner along with a private room that holds up to 50 people for special occasions or business meetings for reservations please call 816-942-8870.

Lobster Chowder

1 lb. Bacon, Med Dice	2 ea. Onion, Med Dice
1 Bunch Celery, Med Dice	3 ea. Carrots, Med Dice
2 lb. Potatoes, Med Dice	2 Bags Corn, Frozen
4 T. Garlic, Minced	1 Can Tomatoes, Whole Peeled
2 Gal. Lobster Stock	1 Can Clam Juice
1 Cup Lemon Juice	2 Cups White Wine
1/2 Cup Parsley, Fresh Chopped	3 T. Oregano, Fresh Chopped
2 T. Black Pepper	2 T. Blackening Seasoning
5 ea. Bay Leaves	Roux

Directions

Dice and sauté bacon, onion, celery, carrot and potatoes in soup kettle. Add corn, garlic and continue to sauté till tender. Add tomatoes, stock and clam juice. Continue to simmer. Add lemon juice and fresh chopped herbs, pepper, bay leaf. Continue to simmer until potatoes are tender and thicken with roux.

Submitted by EBT

FAMOUS DAVE'S LEGENDARY PIT BAR-B-QUE

Legendary Pit Bar-B-Que®

1320 Village West Parkway
Kansas City, KS 66111
(913) 334-8646
Fax (913) 334-0700

FAMOUS DAVE'S THOUGHTS ON COOKING

To me, the most important part of creating food that is tasty, full-flavored, and memorable is relentless attention to details: flavor and texture profiles, plus how good something smells while cooking or being served. Early on when I started fooling around with my first barbeque sauces, I quickly realized I didn't know a thing about seasonings. I wasn't at all familiar with herbs, spices, or natural flavorings. I didn't know what they looked like, how they tasted, or how to use them, much less how to pronounce most of them. And, the more I cook, the more I realize how much I don't know.

I cringe when I seek folks just grabbing any ingredient off the shelf when cooking a recipe. Often, I see shoppers in the grocery store wondering which product of the huge variety to buy. The only way to know is to buy them all, taste them all, and keep notes on the taste differences. When developing a recipe which calls for mustard, I will buy every mustard available to discover which has the right flavor profile that will make the recipe I'm working on outstanding. For example, over the years, I have identified the best-tasting Worcestershire sauces, mustards, apricot jams, and so on. Even the same seasoning from another manufacturer will taste different.

Creamy Sweet & Sour Coleslaw

10 Cups chopped shredded red and green cabbage

1/4 Cup grated carrot	2 Cups Miracle Whip
1/2 Cup sugar	2 Tbsp. prepared horseradish
1 Tbsp. dry mustard	1 Tbsp. white pepper
1/2 Tsp. salt	1/4 Tsp. garlic powder
1/4 Tsp. celery seeds	

Directions

Toss the cabbage and carrot in a bowl. Mix salad dressing, sugar, horseradish, dry mustard, white pepper, salt, garlic powder and celery seeds in a bowl. Add to cabbage mixture and mix well. Chill, covered until serving time.

Yields 6 to 8 servings.

Submitted by Famous Dave

HAYWARD'S PIT BAR-B-QUE

11051 Antioch Rd.
Overland Park, KS
(913) 451-8080

We are a family owned and operated authentic barbeque restaurant founded on August 19, 1972. Hayward's offers the finest state of the art in barbequing. Only the highest quality of meats are carefully selected and seasoned and most of our side dishes are made right here at Hayward's.

We offer the finest in catering services. Let Hayward's make your next get together perfect by catering your business meeting or social party any place within the greater Kansas City area. No group is too large or too small. Just call our catering department for details at (913) 451-8080, Monday through Friday, 9:00AM-4:00PM.

Potato Salad

(Yields 10 4-oz. servings)
Peel and steam (until tender) or boil approximately 1 hour and then peel 2 lbs. of potatoes (red or white). Dice in 1/2-in. to 3/4-in. cubes and chill.
Mix together the following and add to potatoes:

1/2 Cup Dill Pickle
1 Large Chopped Onion
Salt and pepper to taste.

2 Tbsp. Prepared Mustard
3/4 Cup Mayonnaise

Cole Slaw

(Yields 10 4-oz. servings)
Chop finely or shred the following: 1 head cabbage, 1 large carrot
Thoroughly mix into the Coleslaw Dressing.

Coleslaw Dressing:

1-1/4 Cup Kraft Cuisine Dressing
1 Tbsp. Wine Vinegar
1 Tsp. Dry Mustard (Ground)

3 Tbsp. Buttermilk
1 Tsp. Monosodium Glutamate
Pinch of Granulated Garlic

Submitted by Hayward Spears

IVY'S RESTAURANT

240 N. E. Barry Road
Kansas City, MO 64155
(816) 436-3320
Fax (816) 436-3329

Ivy's was started in 1977 by Sam and Carol Cross. We offer Poultry, Steaks, Prime Rib, Seafood and Pasta. The Pasta Kitchen is a favorite entree to have when visiting Ivy's. The chef prepares the dish with one of your favorite sauces, pasta and many vegetables and meat choices. You can make it spicy, with lots of garlic or as plain as you want.

We also offer live jazz on Friday and Saturday from 6:30 p.m. to 10 p.m. This is a separate dining area in the restaurant. We also offer private dining rooms for 8 to 80. Ivy's was voted the most romantic restaurant in the Northland and received many awards for food and wine.

Steak Soup

2 lb. Hamburger	1 lb. Cubed Prime Rib
1 Onion, Diced	4 oz. Butter
1 Tbsp. Cavenders	1/4 Cup Flour
3 Small Cans Stew Vegetables	1 Tbsp. Garlic
1 Tbsp. Kitchen Bouquet	1/2 Cup Beef Broth
1 Cup Water	Salt & Pepper to Taste

Directions

In stock pot add butter, onion, burger and prime rib. Cook until browned. Add flour and cook 5 minutes. Add the rest of the ingredients. Bring to a boil, then turn down to a simmer and let simmer for an hour.

Submitted by Ivy's Restaurant

JASPER'S RESTAURANT

1201 W. 103rd Street
Kansas City, MO 64114
(816) 941-6600
Fax (816) 941-4346

Jasper's, Kansas City's oldest and most authentic Italian Restaurant has been open at our new location in Watts Mill in south Kansas City for over 6 years now. For 50 years Jasper's has continued its award-winning dedication to fine Italian Cuisine and impeccable service. The menu features our famous Scampi Alla Livornese, Caesar Salad, Fresh Pastas, Veal, Steaks, and Chops as well as Fresh Seafood and Homemade Bread and Pastries. The new "Enoteca" Wine Bar features over 400 wines from Italy with many being served by the glass. The bar also features the city's largest selection of fine distilled spirits, Grappas and Espresso Coffee Drinks. Jasper and Leonard, in following with their father's legacy of dedication to fine Italian Cuisine and service have resulted in Jasper's being the most awarded restaurant in Kansas City's history.

Jasper Jr.'s Pasta Fagioli (Tuscan Bean Soup)

1 16 oz. Northern White or Cannellini Beans
1 Whole Diced Carrots
1/2 Tsp. Salt
1/2 Tsp. Red Pepper
1-1/2 Cups Ditali Pasta
6-8 Chopped San Marzano Tomatoes
4 oz. Diced Pancetta
2 Whole Diced Celery
1 Whole Diced Medium Onion
1/2 Tsp. Ground Black Pepper
8 oz. Olive Oil
6 Cups Chicken Broth
2 Cloves Minced Garlic

Directions

Soak the beans overnight in cold water. Heat 1/2 cup olive oil in a large sauté pan and add onions, carrots, garlic, celery and pancetta. Sauté for several minutes. Pour broth into large pot and add vegetables and pancetta and beans. Add seasonings and tomatoes. Cook for 1-1/2 hours. Add escarole or spinach, cook pasta in separate pot. Drain and add to soup. Then drizzle in the other 1/2 cup of olive oil Serve very hot. Serves 8-10.

Submitted by Jasper

KC MASTERPIECE BARBECUE & GRILL

I-435 & Metcalf
Overland Park, KS 66215
(913) 345-1199

On the Country Club Plaza
47th & Wyandotte
Kansas City, MO
(816) 531-7111

KC Masterpiece® Barbecue and Grill serves outstanding, authentic barbecue and other smoked meats in combination with original, premium side-dishes and desserts. An emphasis on authentic barbecue cooking distinguishes KC Masterpiece® Restaurants from their competition. At the restaurants all meat is grilled or smoked using 100% hickory wood. While barbecue is the featured offering, the restaurants also offer homemade soups, salads, grilled chicken, fish and premium steaks. Many of these original items like Onion Straws, Doc's Dip, KCM Baked Beans and the Chocolate Peanut Butter Ice Cream Pie have received the praise of customers and press alike for their mouth-watering flavors for over 18 years.

Crispy & Crunchy Chilled Veggie Salad

MARINADE
1/2 Cup Apple Cider Vinegar
1 Cup White Sugar
1 Tsp. Finely Ground Black Pepper
1/2 Cup Vegetable Oil
1/2 Tsp. Coarse Salt
1 Packet Original Hidden Valley Ranch Dressing

Place all ingredients in small sauce pan and bring to a low boil, stirring constantly.

VEGGIES
2 lbs. of fresh vegetables (carrots, celery, onion, red & green peppers, etc.) equal parts of each.

Chop vegetables into small pieces. Place vegetables in a shallow heat proof dish. Slowly pour hot marinade over vegetables, stirring to coat. Cover with plastic and refrigerate several hours or overnight. Can be kept refrigerated for several days.

Submitted KC Masterpiece Barbecue & Grill

KC MASTERPIECE BARBECUE & GRILL

I-435 & Metcalf
Overland Park, KS 66215
(913) 345-1199

On the Country Club Plaza
47th & Wyandotte
Kansas City, MO
(816) 531-7111

KC Masterpiece® Barbecue and Grill serves outstanding, authentic barbecue and other smoked meats in combination with original, premium side-dishes and desserts. An emphasis on authentic barbecue cooking distinguishes KC Masterpiece® Restaurants from their competition. At the restaurants all meat is grilled or smoked using 100% hickory wood. While barbecue is the featured offering, the restaurants also offer homemade soups, salads, grilled chicken, fish and premium steaks. Many of these original items like Onion Straws, Doc's Dip, KCM Baked Beans and the Chocolate Peanut Butter Ice Cream Pie have received the praise of customers and press alike for their mouth-watering flavors for over 18 years.

Smoked Turkey Salad

Delicious served on fresh salad greens, in half a cantaloupe, or on good-quality bread as a sandwich filling, this recipe makes plain old chicken salad taste pretty tame.

2-1/4 Cups Bite-sized Pieces of Smoke Turkey
4 Hard-Boiled Eggs, Chopped Fine
2 Tbsp. Dijon Mustard
1 Jalapeno Pepper, Diced
1 Tsp. Black Pepper
1 Cup Chopped Red Onion
2 Cups Mayonnaise
1 Tsp. Celery Salt
1 Tsp. White Pepper
1 Tsp. Ground Cumin

Directions

Combine turkey, onion, and eggs. In a separate bowl, combine mayonnaise with remaining ingredients. Add mayonnaise mixture to turkey mixture and blend well. Refrigerate until ready to serve. Serves 6-8.

Submitted by KC Masterpiece Barbecue & Grill

K.T. FRYER'S

Dine In • Carry Out • Catering

12842 W. 87th Parkway, Lenexa, KS 66215
(913) 894-0800

Hours:
Mon.-Fri. 11 a.m. - 10 p.m. • Sat. 4 p.m. - 10 p.m.
Sun. 11 a.m. - 9 p.m.
Reservations Accepted for 6 or More

The best kept secret in Lenexa is at 12842 W. 87th Parkway. In July 1991 Kurtis Lam opened the doors with the idea of pan fried chicken like Grandma did on Sundays. 13 years later we might not be the Best Kept Secret anymore, but it's still the best chicken in town. We are a family style restaurant serving food made from scratch. Our menu includes a variety of foods such as sandwiches, catfish, pork chops.

See you soon.

Homemade Chicken Noodle Soup

5 gal. water	1 lb. chicken base
2 stalks celery (diced)	2 yellow onions
6 medium carrots	1/2 tsp. yellow food coloring
1 tsp. white pepper	6 pieces raw chicken (your choice)
2 - 3 lb. bags of noodles	

Directions

Add above ingredients to water. Heat to boil then add your noodles. Cook noodles until they are done. Then remove from heat and remove chicken. Then dice chicken and put diced chicken back in soup. Simmer and serve.

Submitted by Shelbin Chatman

MALONEY'S SPORTS BAR & GRILL

7201 W. 79th
Overland Park, KS 66204
(913) 385-9595
Fax (913) 385-9363

This friendly, neighborhood sports bar and grill offers something for everyone. The menu features a variety of delicious options including homemade soups, sandwiches and pizzas or calzones. Sports fans can watch any event on ne of the 20 televisions. Patrons can also enjoy fresh air and cold beverages on our spacious patio.

Italian Vegetable with Sausage

1 1b. Cooked Italian Sausage
5-1/2 qts. Water
2 Cups Large Diced Celery
1 Large Yellow Squash, Large Diced
12-15 Cloves of Garlic, Minced
Sugar (to take the tartness out)

6 lbs. Canned Tomatoes
2 Cups Large Diced Carrots
2 Cups Large Diced Yellow Onions
1 Zucchini, Large Diced
Salt, Pepper, Basil, Oregano to taste
Oil (enough to cover vegetables)

Directions

In a large soup pot sauté the vegetables in oil over medium-high heat for about 3-5 minutes. Add garlic and sauté for a couple minutes longer. Puree tomato and combine with water and spices. Add to soup pot when veggies are somewhat soft. Add chopped Italian sausage and simmer so that flavors develop. You could add mini meatballs instead of sausage or leave out the meat for a vegetarian soup.

Submitted by Steve Martini

MARRAKESH CAFÉ

7528 W. 119th Street
Overland Park, KS 66213
(913) 661-0500
www.marrakeshcafe.com

Marrakesh Café is one-of-a-kind in the Greater Kansas City area. Here you can experience a combination of Moroccan and Mediterranean cuisine. Our buffet offers a wonderful selection of famous Moroccan and Mediterranean dishes such as Cous Cous, Tagine, Gyro Lamb, Falafil Hummus, Grape Leaves, Chicken, Beef, Salmon, Baklava and much more.

Tabouleh (Salad)

3 Branches of parsley
3 Fresh lemons
1 Tbs. Salt
4 Large Tomatoes

2 Tbs. Cous Cous
2 Tbs. Olive oil
3 Leaves of fresh mint

Directions

Soak Cous Cous for 15 minutes in warm water. Chop parsley fine. Mix parsley with Cous Cous and chop tomato and add squeezed fresh lemons and olive oil. Add salt and mint. Chop. Mix everything. Enjoy!

Submitted by Mustapha Alhiane

O'NEILL'S RESTAURANT & BAR

4016 W. 95th Street
Priarie Village, KS 66207
(913) 648.4900

O'Neill's opened in March 2000, The owner Brian Schorgl was born and raised in Kansas City. Brian's desire was to open a restaurant in his neighborhood that people could meet with friends and family for a good homemade meal.

O'Neill's Cobb Salad

3 cups mixed greens (your favorite)
1/2 cup seasoned corn (dash of sugar, pepper, lawrys salt)
1/4 cup sliced red onion   5 sliced red peppers
1/2 cup avocado sliced
6 oz poached chicken (allow to cool after cooked, then shred with fingers)
2 hard boiled eggs (chopped)   1/2 cup alfalfa sprouts

Directions

Place mixed greens in a bowl top with all ingredients in order of recipe be sure to crown your salad with the alfalfa sprouts

Serve with your favorite dressing.

Submitted by Bonnie Hall

PIERPONT'S

Fresh Seafood • Prime Steaks

Located in Union Station
(816) 221-5111 • www.pierponts.com

Named for the railroad baron, J.P. (John Pierpont) Morgan, Pierpont's 1914 decor combined with 21st century innovation offers you old world elegance with contemporary flair.

This is your very special invitation to experience Pierpont's at Union Station. It's been dubbed "the culinary jewel" of Kansas City's historically renovated Union Station, and has earned the reputation of serving Kansas City's finest steak and seafood selections.

As a sister restaurant to the legendary Hereford House, Pierpont's maintains the family tradition of serving prime steak, perfectly aged and prepared. With fresh seafood arriving daily, an award winning wine list, and the unique creations of some of the areas finest chefs, Pierpont's has been named "Best Place to Entertain Guests" and "Best Place to take a Group" from the local press.

In addition to dining room seating, your smaller party will enjoy the private Wine Cellar rooms, while larger banquets overlook the grand dining room below. Reservations are always honored, but not required. www.herefordhouse.com

Pierpont's Walla Walla Onion Soup

1 Tbsp. Butter, unsalted
4 Onions, Large, Walla Walla (or other sweet variety), thinly sliced
4-3/4 Cups Chicken stock
1 Tsp. Sea salt, finely ground (or to taste)
Black pepper, fresh ground: 4 Turns (of the peppermill, or to taste)
3/4 Tsp. Thyme, fresh, minced

1/2 Teaspoon Garlic, freshly minced
3 Tbsp Port wine.
3 Tbsp. Sherry wine.
1-1/2 Cups Veal glaze (demi-glace reduced by half)

3/4 Tsp. Oregano, fresh, minced

Directions

Place the butter in a large, heavy-bottomed pot and turn on medium heat. When the butter melts, foams and subsides, add the sliced onions and garlic. Slowly caramelize the onions until deep brown, but not burnt. Turn down the heat if it looks like the onions are about to burn. Stir frequently to promote even caramelization.

When the onions are done, deglaze the pan with the sherry and port wines. Reduce by half, and then add the chicken stock and veal glaze. Stir well to incorporate, bring to a boil, then turn down the heat and simmer for five minutes to allow the flavors to meld.

Turn off the heat and add the fresh herbs, salt and pepper. Allow to sit for two minutes to incorporate, then stir and serve.

SERVICE:

Walla Walla onion soup: 8 Fluid Ounces

Comté cheese (or Swiss gruyere or appenzeller), sliced thin: 1 Ounce (enough to cover)

Crostini (or toasts, really, of any kind): 2 Each (enough to cover)

Chives, thinly sliced: For garnish

Preheat a broiler or oven at 450°F. Ladle the hot onion soup into an oven-safe bowl. Add the crostinis and top with the comté cheese. Make sure the entire surface is well covered with cheese, and then place into the oven, or under the broiler. Cook until the cheese melts and starts to brown. Then garnish with chives and enjoy!   *Submitted by Pierpont's*

11801 College Blvd.
Overland Park, KS 66210
(913) 460-8405
Fax (913) 469-4222

This intimate little hideaway is the perfect spot to enjoy a quiet dinner and some spectacular wines. The traditional Italian cuisine is complemented by exotic chef specialties as well as wood-fired pizzas. The great value wine list includes many family owned boutique wines imported by Small Vineyards from Italy. Our patio lounge seating is perfect for savoring a martini and an appetizer.

Strawberry Spinach Salad with Raspberry Vinaigrette

Raspberry vinaigrette - serves 4
1/2 c. raspberry sugar
1 lb. spinach
Pinch dry tarragon
3/4 c. frozen raspberries
1/2 pt. fresh strawberries

Roasted pine nuts
Pinch dry thyme
1/4 lb. brown sugar
1/4 c. Gorgonzola cheese
1 c. olive oil

Directions

In bowl combine spinach and strawberries, set aside. Using a blender combine herbs, raspberries, vinegar, brown sugar and oil, blend until smooth. Toss with fresh salad mixture, top with Gorgonzola cheese and pine nuts.

Submitted by Chef Kelli Billingsley

SAY CHEESE

grilled fresh to order

Gourmet Grilled Cheese Sandwiches

11149 W. 95th Street
Overland Park, KS 66214
(913) 307-2020
Fax (913) 307-0055

Try an new experience in dining at The Oak Park Mall (next to Nordstrom's lower entrance). "Say Cheese", a grilled cheese sandwich with a bowl of hot tomato soup, just like mom used to make. Or try any of our fresh sandwiches, soups and salads. Everything made fresh daily. Come give us a try and "Say Cheese!"

Spinach Salad w/Kiwi Poppy Seed Dressing

1 lb. Fresh Spinach
Red Onions
Dressing:
3 Tsp. Sugar
2 Tsp. Chopped Yellow Onions
1/4 Cup Salad Oil
Salt & Pepper to Taste

3 Med. Strawberries
Toasted Almonds

1 Tsp. Dry Mustard
1/2 Cup Rice Wine Vinegar
1 Egg
1 Tsp. Poppy Seeds

Directions

In large bowl place spinach, slice strawberries, almonds, sliced red onion. Set to the side.

In a blender add all of the dressing ingredients except poppy seeds, salad oil and egg. Blend on high until smooth. Add eggs. Then slowly add salad oil. It should get thick and smooth. Fold in poppy seeds. Dress salad with dressing.

Submitted by David Kovich

SUNG SON A VIETNAMESE BISTRO

SUNG SON
Vietnamese Bistro

4116-4118 Pennsylvania Ave.
Kansas city, Mo 64111
(816) 931-0670
Mon-Fri: 11 a.m-10p.m
Sun : 12 p.m -9 p.m

Looking for a quick lunch of soup, an exquisite vegetarian meal, exotic ingredients, or perhaps something healthy ? Why not think VIETNAMESE?

SUNG SON A VIETNAMESE BISTRO is a great new find for authentic VIETNAMESE food in Kansas City, MO. Experience traditional favorite like the soup PHO, the vermicelli BUN dishes or try our fresh, healthy vegetarian specialties. Select from our menu or make a special request for you, or your family.

Chicken Salad (Servings 4-6)

1 lb. chicken breast
Juice of 2 limes or lemons
4 sprigs cilantro
from
2 red bird's eye chilies, thinly sliced
4 tbsp. chopped unsalted roasted peanuts
1 medium-sized carrot, peeled & shredded

4 tbsp. sugar
3 cloves garlic, minced
4 sprigs Asian basil, strip leaves

their stems, sliced
1 head cabbage, shredded
1 medium-size daikon, peeled and
    shredded (optional)

Directions

Boil the chicken breast around 30 minutes, and then let it cool enough to handle, cut into thin slices.

Meanwhile, in a small bowl, whisk together the lime juice, fish sauce, and sugar in a bowl until the sugar is completely dissolved. Add the garlic, and chili and let marinade stand for 5 minutes.

Toss the slice chicken breast with cabbage, carrot, daikon and basil with the marinade.

Finish with the cilantro and crushed peanut in the top

Submitted by SUNG SON

WAID'S FAMILY RESTAURANTS

**6920 Mission Rd.
Prairie Village, KS
(913) 362-2882**

**1130 W. 103rd
Kansas City, MO
(816) 942-1354**

Our tradition of quality, service and value began in 1953. Serving breakfast, lunch and dinner for over 50 years, we start with the highest quality ingredients preparing our own original recipes right on the premises. Great home style foods served in a friendly, comfortable atmosphere is what makes Waid's value greater than ever.

Cheese Soup

2-1/4 qts. Water
3-1/4 oz. Green pepper
3-1/4 oz. Onion
3/4 oz. Salt
6-1/2 oz. Roux
40 oz. Milk
3/4 cup Water

3-1/4 oz. Carrots
3-1/4 oz. Celery
1/2 tbsp. White pepper
1 tbsp. Chicken base
1 lb. Sharp cheddar cheese
1 oz. Corn starch

Directions

Place water, vegetables and seasonings in a large stainless steel stock pot. Bring to a boil and cook for 1/2 hour. Whip in roux until thick and evenly blended and brought to a boil.

In a double boiler, place milk and cheese. Stir frequently. As soon as milk is hot and cheese is melted, add corn starch/water mixture, whip and remove from stove. When both pots are ready, pour the milk and cheese mixture into veggie mixture and blend well. Serve and enjoy. Makes 1 gallon.

Submitted by Paul D. Russell

Restaurant Recipes of

ENTRÉES

810 ZONE

4800 W. 119th Street
Leawood KS 66209
(913) 469-ZONE

810 Zone is unlike any other restaurant in the Kansas City area. We offer a new and exciting dining experience with a live broadcast booth on site for Sports Radio 810. With a full bar and menu, how could you go wrong? Check out the interactive TVs, sports memorabilia and of course, the daily live radio broadcasts.

Smoked Beef Brisket

2 cans Dr. Pepper
3 oz. Balsamic Vinegar
6 oz. Salad oil
5 oz. Franks Red Hot Sauce

Favorite Spice Rub
1 lg. Brisket
Apple and Hickory Wood

Directions

Whisk all ingredients together.

Pour marinade over the brisket. Cover with plastic wrap and refrigerate for 24 hours. Turn occasionally.

Drain marinade and pat brisket dry. Rub with favorite spices.

Place brisket in smoker with a constant temperature of 175 -225 degrees. Smoke 1 hour per pound of meat. Internal temperature should read 200 degrees when done. Cool and slice. Serve as deserved.

Submitted by K.C. Hopps, Ltd.

AUSTINS BAR & GRILL

Carry Out Available
829-2106
151 & Mur-Len Olathe Kansas
"A fine beer may be judged with only one sip,
but it is better to be thoroughly sure."

Austins Bar & Grill has been a local favorite since it was established in 1987. Known for Steaks, Ribs and Burgers, Austins customers come hungry and leave satisfied. One of Austin's most popular dishes is the chicken fried steak.

Chicken Fried Steak

1 lb. Boneless Beef Top Loin
1 Egg, Beaten
Salt & Pepper to Taste
1 Cup All Purpose Flour
1 Qt. Buttermilk

2 Cups Shortening
1 Cup Buttermilk
1/4 Tsp. Garlic Powder
1/4 Cup All Purpose Flour
Salt & Pepper to Taste

Directions

Cut top loin crosswise into 4 (4 oz.) cutlets. Pound cutlet with a mallet.

In a large skillet heat 1/2 inch shortening to 365 degrees. While shortening is heating, prepare cutlets. In a shallow bowl, beat together eggs, buttermilk, salt and pepper. In another shallow dish mix garlic powder and 1 cup flour. Dip cutlets into flour, turning to evenly coat both sides. Dip in egg mixture, coating both sides, then in flour mixture once again.

Place cutlets in heated shortening. Cook until golden brown, turning once. Transfer to plate lined with paper towels. Repeat with remaining cutlets. Drain grease, reserving 1/2 cup.

Using the reserved drippings in the pan, prepare gravy over medium heat. Blend in 1/4 cup flour to form paste. Gradually add milk to desired consistency, stirring constantly. Heat through and salt and pepper to taste. Serve with chicken fried steak.

Submitted by Joseph Happold

BIRDIES PUB & GRILL

**8889 W. 75th Street
Overland Park, KS 66204
(913) 648-4011
Fax (913) 381-8117**

"Better Than Par"

Birdies Pub & Grill established in 1985, offers a wide variety of menu options including sandwiches, steaks, pizzas, and daily homemade lunch specials. Birdies is "all sports all the time" with 16 TVs, 2 Jumbo Screens featuring the NFL Ticket in the Fall. We offer wireless internet access, a large game room, and a separate party room for your next special occasion. We look forward to seeing you at Birdies Pub & Grill where we are "Better Than Par."

Beef Stroganoff with Noodles

This recipe is our family favorite. The sauce is very rich and creamy and is great served over egg noodles. It does take a little longer to make, but it is well worth it! Prep Time: approx. 20 minutes. Cook Time: approx. 1 hour 30 minutes. Ready in: approx. 2 hours. Original recipe makes 6 servings. Recipe has been scaled to make 20 servings.

1 tbsp. vegetable oil	3/4 cup and 1 tbsp. & 1 tsp. cornstarch
2 lbs. beef stew meat, cut into 1/2-in. pieces	10 (14 oz.) cans beef broth
1 lb. bacon, cut into 1/2-in. pieces	3-1/4 (8 oz.) pkgs. dry egg noodles
1 onion, diced	1 tbsp. & 1/4 tsp. butter
1 tbsp. seasoning salt	6-3/4 (4 oz.) cans sliced mushrooms
3/4 cup and 1 tbsp. & 1 tsp. Worcestershire sauce	1 cup and 1 tbsp. cold water
3 1/4 (8 oz.) containers sour cream	

Directions

In a large Dutch oven heat the oil over high heat and brown the cubed stew meat. Remove from pan. In the same pan, sauté the bacon and onion until onions are translucent and bacon is fully cooked. Return the browned stew meat to the pan.

Stir in seasoning salt, Worcestershire sauce and beef broth. Bring to a boil, then cover and reduce the heat to medium. Simmer for 1 to 1 1/2 hours or until meat is fork tender.

Bring a large pot of lightly salted water to a boil. Add the egg noodles and cook for 8 to 10 minutes or until al dente; drain.

In a skillet, melt the butter over medium heat and sauté the mushrooms for 3 to 4 minutes. Add the mushrooms to the meat mixture.

Bring the meat mixture to a boil. Mix together the cornstarch and the water, and stir into the meat mixture.

Submitted by Rick & Michelle

BO LINGS

Plaza Board of Trade
48th & Main • (816) 753-1718

Orchard Corner Center
95th & Quivira • (913) 888-6618

Gateway Plaza
91st & Metcalf • (913) 341-1718

Overland Park
135th & Metcalf • (913) 239-8188

www.bolings.com

Owners Richard and Theresa Ng do extensive research to ensure that all items on the menu, even the rice (a blend of aromatic jasmine long grain rice and fluffy American long grain rice), is the best available. "It is our goal to provide good, healthy food with the best service, so there is plenty of time to enjoy your meal, and sit and talk and drink tea with friends. It's part of the Chinese tradition," says Richard Ng. Local publications have named Bo Lings best Chinese restaurant in Kansas City time and again. Recently, Bo Lings was named one of the top 100 Chinese restaurants in America by national publication Chinese Restaurant News!

Shitake Mushrooms with Greens

1/2 lb. Shitake Mushrooms
3 Cloves Garlic
2 Tbsp. Soy Sauce
A Little Stock or Water
1 Tbsp. Cornstarch

1/2 lb. Baby Bok Choy
1 Tsp. Chopped Fresh Ginger
1 Tsp. Sugar
Vegetable Oil
2 Tsp. Sesame Seed Oil

Directions

Blanche the bok choy and arrange on the bottom of serving dish. Then stir -fry the ginger and garlic in a little bit of vegetable oil. Add the mushrooms, stock and soy sauce, and simmer for 10 minutes. Thicken sauce with cornstarch, then add sesame seed oil. Place atop the bok choy. Delicious!

Submitted by Richard Ng, Owner/Chef of Bo Lings Fine Chinese Cuisine

BUGATTI'S RISTORANTE & CAFE

AMERISTAR CASINO & HOTEL
Bugatti's Ristorante & Cafe
3200 North Ameristar Drive, Kansas City, MO 64161
(800) 499-4961 or (816) 414-7000

The Bugatti is one of classiest automobiles ever made, and Bugatti's Ristorante & Café ranks as one of the best restaurants in Kansas City. Created to honor the legacy of excellence established by the Bugatti family a century ago, Bugatti's puts a fresh spin on traditional Italian cuisine with an inspired menu of pasta, pizza, fish, veal and steaks.

Start with an appetizer of lobster ravioli or fire-roasted mussels, and follow it up with a comforting bowl of minestrone soup or one of Bugatti's fresh salads. After that, there's still plenty of time to enjoy a delicious pizza, pasta, grilled panini or one of Bugatti's Café specialties like a chef's choice risotto or Chicken Parmesan. For meat and seafood lovers, there is an extensive choice of steaks, chops, filets, and fresh seafood dishes on offer. Of special note are two alluring veal dishes, including a delicate Veal Marsala, and a superb rack of lamb.

Spaghettini al Cartoccio

Spaghettini al Cartoccio, literally means "pasta in a bag." It is a unique way to prepare many items, not just pasta. Fish and chicken are great when prepared this way.

Yield one serving

8 oz. Spaghetti, Cooked
2 ea. Sea Scallops
4 ea. Fresh Mussels
2 oz. Crab Meat
3 oz. Fish Fumet (clam juice can be used)
1 Tsp. Fresh Oregano

3 ea. Raw Jumbo Shrimp, Peeled & Deveined
4 ea. Fresh Clams
3 oz. Calamari Cleaned and Cut
8 oz. Marinara Sauce
1 Tsp. Fresh Basil
1 Piece Parchment Paper, 24 x16

Directions

Combine the marinara and the fish fumet or clam juice. Toss the cooked pasta and all of the seafood together gently with the herbs and sauce. Fold the parchment paper in half then unfold. Place the pasta mixture on one half and fold the other half over. Then starting in once corner fold the edges of the paper as to create a seal, making a semi circular pouch or bag.

Place cartoccio in oven-safe pan, drizzle a little olive oil on the top of the paper and place in a 350 degree oven for approximately 15 to 18 minutes. The bag will puff up and brown.

Submitted by Edward Allen, Executive Chef

CAFÉ ITALIA

8603 North Oak Trafficway
Kansas City, MO 64155
(816) 468-5800

Café Italia is Kansas City's premier Italian restaurant offering homemade Italian bread, salads, soups, meat, chicken, seafood, pasta and pizza dishes. Café Italia has a full service bar/lounge, Espresso bar, banquet facility and outdoor patio. Open 7 days a week. Reservations accepted.

Bistecca Fra Diavolo

4 Peeled fresh tomatoes
1 Small white onion
1 Tsp. salt
1/4 Cup Olive oil

2 Tbsp. Fresh or dry hot red peppers
2 Tbsp. fresh chopped garlic (fine)
1 lb. Beef tenderloin slice in 3/4"
   medallions

Directions

In a sauté pan, place olive oil, red pepper, garlic, salt and onion (chopped). Sauté on medium high heat until garlic browns. Chop the whole tomato and place in pan with all juice, add 1/2 cup of water. Grill meat on high heat on oven broiler or sear in hot pan until reaching desired cooking temperature. Place sauce on a large platter and place meat on top. Serve hot.

Submitted by Guy Tamburello, Chef

Café Maison

408 E. 63rd Street
Kansas City, MO 64110
(816) 523-3400 Fax (816) 523-3633
www.cafemaisonkc.com

Hours
Sunday Brunch from 10 a.m. to 2 p.m.
Lunch: Tuesday through Saturday 11 a.m. to 2:30 p.m.
Dinner: Tuesday through Saturday 5:30 p.m. to 9 p.m.

Café Maison is a colorful, cozy restaurant oozing French Country, with the look and feel of a neighborhood bistro plucked straight from a Parisian street corner. Proprietor Jeffrey Fitzpatrick originally opened this intimate restaurant in 1999. It bustles during midday where signature dishes such as rich tomato-basil soup, tender crepes, fresh creative salads, flavorful quiches and citrus-laden lemon cake, have created a loyal following of luncheon regulars. Enjoy Café Maison for dinner, come in and enjoy the candlelit French dining room. Savor an appetizer of French Country Paté or a Blue Cheese Savory Tarte. Delight your taste buds with Lamb Chops, Salmon Encrouté, or a Halibut Filet drizzled with a Tarragon Cream Sauce as examples of dinner entrées.

Trout with Fennel

6 Rainbow Trout, Cleaned   Olive Oil
3 Fennel Bulbs, Trimmed, Cored, and Finely Sliced
1-1/2 Cups Grated Parmesan   Salt
Pepper   1/3 Cup Heavy Cream
1/3 Cup White Wine

Directions

Heat the oven to 350 degrees. Rinse the trout under cold water and dry with paper towels. Place on a large lightly oiled baking sheet.

Lightly oil a large baking dish and layer the fennel with half of the parmesan, seasoning each layer with salt and pepper. Pour the cream and white wine over the top and sprinkle with the remaining parmesan.

Cover the fennel dish with aluminum foil and bake for 20 minutes. Then remove the foil and bake for 10 minutes. Add the fish to the fennel and bake for 20 minutes.

Serve the fish on a bed of fennel. Serves 6.

Submitted by Jeffrey Fitzpatrick

CALLAHAN'S PIZZERIA • PUB • GRILL

12843 W. 87th St. Parkway
Lenexa, KS
(913) 894-1717

Home to Those Who've Been Kicked Out of Theirs!

For nearly fifteen years Callahan's has been "home to those who've been kicked out of theirs." Callahans was founded in 1991.

Callahan's can be best described as a "classic neighborhood pub" with an eclectic atmosphere and friendly service. (many of our associates have been employed for more than five years)

Owner Barry Zillner, grew up in the hospitality industry and gained invaluable experience working in several area Gilbert Robinson establishments. Barry has flipped burgers, and poured cocktails in some of the best restaurants in K.C. Callahan's is the culmination of his experience and is why Callahan's is no ordinary bar and grill.

Callahan's offers a made from scratch classic americana menu, Ice cold Beer, Cocktails, and Great daily specials.

Callahan's offers Patio Dining, Big screen TV's, and Video Games. There is something for everyone and Children are welcome.

St. Patrick's Day Corned Beef & Cabbage

1 Good Quality Corned Beef Flat
1 cup yellow mustard (at home we always use up all the half empty specialty mustards in the back of the fridge.)
1 cup packed dark brown sugar
1/2 half tsp. ground cloves

1/2 tsp. ground allspice
1/2 tsp salt

Directions

In a large stock pot, boil the corned beef according to instructions on bag. (about 2 hours) TIP- THE TRICK TO TENDER CORNED BEEF IS TO COOK THE DAYLIGHTS OUT OF IT. WHEN YOU THINK ITS DONE THROW IT BACK IN THE POT AND LET IT COOK FOR ANOTHER HOUR. Let the corned beef cool and slice into 1/4 inch slices. Place the sliced corned beef in a 9x9 baking dish and set aside.

In a medium saucepan, add the mustard, brown sugar, and spices and heat thoroughly until brown sugar dissolves into the mustard.

Pour the mustard sauce over the sliced corned beef and place in a 350 degree oven for 45 minutes to an hour.

Serve with boiled potatoes and cabbage.

An ice cold Smithwicks Irish Ale goes excellent with this dish!!

Submitted by Barry Zillner

CHELLY'S CAFE

218 West 85th St.
(85th & Wornall)
Kansas City, MO
(816) 237-1052
Fax (816) 237-1110

Ruben and Norma Campos are the owners of two little restaurants, The first, Chelly's Cafe is located at 85th St. and Wornall Rd. The second, Don Ruby's Taqueria, is located in DeSoto, Kansas which will serve original dishes from Zacatecas, Mexico.

With a familiar atmosphere as well as the recipes made from scratch, our menu includes, tamales, fajitas, enchiladas, burritos and our signature dish "chiles rellenos", which is so well known. Also on the weekends we have "live music," "folkloric dances," and much more.

Chiles Rellenos – Poblano Chiles

2 Poblano Chiles
Ground Beef

Favorite White Cheese
Salsa

Directions

Roast the chiles and clean them up inside and out, then fill them with the cheese and ground beef. Cover them with battered eggs and fry them for 3-4 minutes. Put them on a plate, add salsa and cheese on top. Melt the cheese and serve.

Submitted by Ruben Campos

CHICKEN-N-BLUES

235 S.E. Main St.
Lee's Summit, MO
(816) 246-0600

Chicken-N-Blues is located in the historic shopping district in Downtown Lee's Summit. We offer pan fried chicken just like a country grandmother would make. Excellent home style country fried steaks, whole catfish and catfish fillets, tender gizzards and livers. Chicken-N-Blues is open Sunday 8 a.m. to 11 a.m. for breakfast and 11 a.m. to 2 p.m. for dinner. Wednesday and Thursday 11 a.m. to 8 p.m. and Friday and Saturday 11 a.m. to 9 p.m. We are closed Monday and Tuesday. Chicken-N-Blues is a non-smoking restaurant.

Country Meatloaf

5 lbs. Ground Beef
4 Whole Eggs
2 Bottles Ketchup
2 Tsp. Italian Seasoning
4 oz. Heinz 57
1/4 Tsp. Oregano
1/2 Cup Brown Sugar

2 Cups Chopped Onions
3 Cups Dry Bread Crumbs
1 Tsp. Garlic Powder
2 Tsp. Worcestershire Sauce
4 oz. A-1 Sauce
1/4 Tsp. Black Pepper

Directions

Mix well. Put in pan and cover with foil.
Bake at 350 degrees for 1 hour 20 minutes.

TOMATO GLAZE: 1 bottle ketchup and 1/4 cup brown sugar. 1 Tsp. Mustard. Remove meatloaf from oven and spread tomato glaze over.

Submitted by Dan Dannaldson

DRAGON INN

OVERLAND PARK
7500 W. 80th Street
(913) 381-7299

CORINTH SQUARE
3975 W. 83rd St.
(913) 381-1688

The Dragon Inn was established in 1975 by Mr. & Mrs. To-Ping Tsui.

In 1974, he moved to Kansas City where he opened the Dragon Inn. The Dragon Inn has now taken its place as one of the finest authentic Chinese restaurants in the greater Kansas City area.

The Dragon Inn is a family-run business. Mr. Tsui and his family work as a team to assure you of the finest service and the very best Chinese food.

The Dragon Inn features authentic Peking and Szechuan dishes. Peking cuisine has been served to royalty in China for many years. Szechuan cuisine is spicy and hot. It is extremely popular in China. These foods are prepared with a specially formulated red pepper sauce and other Chinese herbs.

The Dragon Inn has become a "must" for catering and private parties...and its "Carryout is second to done."

Lemon Chicken

4 Chicken Breasts	1/2 Cup Lemon Juice
1-1/2 Cup Pineapple Juice	2/3 Cup Sugar
1/4 Cup Cornstarch Mixed with Water	1 Lemon Slice

Batter Mix

1-1/2 Cups of All-Purpose Flour	1/2 Cup Cornstarch
1 Egg	1-1/2 Cup of Water
1 Tbsp. of Baking Powder	1 Tbsp. of Salad Oil

Directions

Preparation of Chicken: Pour 4 cups of oil into a frying pan and heat to 350 degree. In a mixing bowl, whip all batter mix ingredients together until smooth. Dip the chicken breasts into the batter mix and put into the heated oil and fry until golden brown. When the chicken breasts are cooked, cut them into 1-inch wide strips and place on a serving dish.

Preparation of Lemon Sauce: Pour 1/2 cup lemon juice, 1-1/2 cup pineapple juice, 1 lemon sliced and 2/3 cup of sugar into a sauce pan and bring to a boil; thicken the sauce with the cornstarch-water mixture until the desired consistency. Pour sauce on top of the sliced chicken breasts and serve.

Submitted by Thomass Tsui

EVERGREEN CHINESE RESTAURANT

Evergreen Chinese Restaurant
Tiblow Centre Shopping Center
13034 Kansas Ave.
Bonner Springs, KS 66012
(913) 441-6484
Fax (913) 441-8880

This place is such a secret treasure. Evergreen Chinese Restaurant in Bonner Springs, KS has settled quietly next to the big city but beats the taste and prices. The people here are so friendly and helpful, the locals come in on a weekly basis to enjoy great Chinese cuisine and friendly service. All food is prepared fresh and cooked to order. Nothing on the menu over $8.95 and lunch specials range from $3.95-$4.95, lunch severed Monday thru Saturday from 11 AM to 3 PM.

Cashew Chicken

Serves 4

1 lb. Boneless Chicken
1/4 lb. Cashews
1/2 Cup Mushrooms
1/2 Cup Carrots

3 Cups Oil for Frying
1 Tsp. Chopped Green Onions
1/2 Cup Chopped Celery

Mixture 1:

1 Tsp. Rice Wine
1 Egg (or 1 Tbsp. Water)

1-1/2 Tbsp. Soy Sauce
2 Tsp. Cornstarch

Mixture 2:

Pinch of Salt
4 Tbsp. Oyster Sauce
1/3 Tsp. Sesame Oil (optional)
3 Tbsp. Cornstarch

3 Tsp. Soy Sauce
1 Tbsp. Sugar
1/2 Cup Water

Directions

Cut the chicken into 1/2" squares. Toss the chicken with Mixture 1 and marinate for at least 30 minutes.

Heat pan and add oil. Heat to 295 degrees. Add the chicken and deep fry for about 1 minutes or until the chicken is done. Remove and drain. Remove all but 4 table-spoons of oil from the pan and reheat until very hot. Add the green onions, celery, carrots and mushrooms, and stir-fry for 1 minute. Add chicken and Mixture 2. Toss lightly to combine the ingredients. Add cashews, cornstarch and toss quickly then remove from the heat. Serve immediately.

Submitted by Evergreen Chinese Restaurant

FAMOUS DAVE'S LEGENDARY PIT BAR-B-QUE

1320 Village West Parkway
Kansas City, KS 66111
(913) 334-8646
Fax (913) 334-0700

FAMOUS DAVE'S THOUGHTS ON COOKING

To me, the most important part of creating food that is tasty, full-flavored, and memorable is relentless attention to details: flavor and texture profiles, plus how good something smells while cooking or being served. Early on when I started fooling around with my first barbeque sauces, I quickly realized I didn't know a thing about seasonings. I wasn't at all familiar with herbs, spices, or natural flavorings. I didn't know what they looked like, how they tasted, or how to use them, much less how to pronounce most of them. And, the more I cook, the more I realize how much I don't know.

I cringe when I seek folks just grabbing any ingredient off the shelf when cooking a recipe. Often, I see shoppers in the grocery store wondering which product of the huge variety to buy. The only way to know is to buy them all, taste them all, and keep notes on the taste differences. When developing a recipe which calls for mustard, I will buy every mustard available to discover which has the right flavor profile that will make the recipe I'm working on outstanding. For example, over the years, I have identified the best-tasting Worcestershire sauces, mustards, apricot jams, and so on. Even the same seasoning from another manufacturer will taste different.

Sloppy Ques

1 lb. ground beef	1/2 C finely chopped sweet yellow onion
1/4 Cup finely chopped green bell pepper	1 jalapeno, finely minced
1 tsp. Famous Dave's steak seasoning	1 Tbsp. chili powder
1/4 tsp. cayenne	1-1/2 Cups Famous Dave's BBQ Sauce
1 tsp. prepared mustard	4 hambuger buns, split, buttered, toasted

Directions

Cook the ground beef in a skillet until the ground beef begins to brown; drain. Stir in onion, green pepper, jalapeno, steak seasoning and chili powder. Cook until the ground beef is cooked through and crumbly, stirring constantly. Add cayenne, sauce and mustard and mix well. Cook until heated through. Spoon onto the buns. Yield 4 servings.

Submitted by Famous Dave

FARRADDAYS' AT ISLE OF CAPRI CASINO

At the Isle of Capri Casino
1800 E. Front St.
Kansas City, MO 64120
(816)855-7777
www.isleofcapricasino.com

Farraddays' Restaurant is located on the welcome deck of the casino. Our Bistro menu showcases certified Angus Beef, wonderful seafood specialties and great appetizers.

Blackened Lobster Tail

1 ea. Lobster Tails
1 oz. Blackening Seasoning
1/2 ea. Avocado
1 oz. Horseradish Cream Sauce

1 oz. Butter, Clarified
3 oz. Mashed Potatoes
1 oz. Beurre Monte
1/2 oz. Chives, Chopped Fine: Garnish

Directions

Place cast iron skillet on medium-high heat and let it get very hot. Take lobster tails and cut completely in half. Remove all of the shell except for the tailpiece. Place clarified butter in shallow dish. Place blackening seasoning in similar dish.

Dredge tails in blackening seasoning, then place tails in clarified butter and immediately place tails in the hot cast iron skillet. Cook for 30 seconds and flip over and cook for another 30 seconds. Ladle a little clarified butter over tails and place in oven for 4-5 minutes until flesh is opaque.

Place 3 oz. of mashed potato in mixing bowl add avocado and mix together with a fork. Place beurre monte on place and swirl on plate until it is evenly covered. Place avocado mashed potatoes in the center of the plate. Spoon or squeeze horseradish cream sauce around mashed potatoes. Remove tails from oven and place directly on top of mashed potatoes. Sprinkle chives around the outside of the plate for a garnish.

Beurre Monte
4 oz. Butter, cold   1 Tbsp. Water
Place water in saucepan and bring to a boil. Remove from heat and whisk until completely incorporated. Stir occasionally to keep from breaking.

Horseradish Cream Sauce
4 oz. Sour Cream   1 oz. Horseradish, grated
TT Salt   1 oz. White Wine
Place sour cream, horseradish, salt and white wine in a mixing bowl. Thoroughly incorporate. Wrap and keep in refrigerator.

Submitted by Farraddays'

GAROZZO'S RISTORANTE

"WHERE CHICKEN SPIEDINI BEGAN"

Garozzo's Ristorante
526 Harrison
Kansas City, MO
(816) 221-2455

Garozzo's Ristorante
2121 N. Webb Road
Wichita, KS
(316) 315-0000

Garozzo's Ristorante &
BanquetRoom
1547 N.E. Rice Road
Lee's Summit, MO
(816) 554-2800

Garozzo's Ristorante
9950 College Blvd.
Overland Park, KS
(913) 491-8300

Garozzo's restaurant was voted Best Ethnic restaurant by Ingram's magazine 2004, Best Italian food by Kansas City magazine 2004 and Zagat rated "Excellent" one of America's top restaurants. Come and enjoy authentic Italian cuisine in a comfortable atmosphere. Michael, his wife Maggie, his four daughters and the entire Garozzo's staff invite you to a true Italian dining experience. Private dining, carry-out and catering available at all locations. Enjoy 1/2 price wine on Sundays, any bottle under $100.00. *Garozzo's Where Chicken Spiedini Began!*

Cavatelli Catania

1 26 oz. jar of Garozzo's Sugo (Sicilian Style Tomato Sauce)
1 1-lb. bag of Cavatelli Pasta
3 tsp. Chopped Garlic
2 Cups Sliced Fresh Mushrooms
1/2 Cup Butter (4 oz.)

1 Cup Diced Red Onions
1 Cup Diced Fresh Tomatoes
2 Cups Chicken Stock
Fresh Grated Romano Cheese

Directions

Cook pasta al dente according to directions on back of package.

Sauté onion and garlic in butter on medium-high heat until brown. Add tomatoes, mushrooms, and cook 2 to 3 minutes. Add Garozzo's Sugo, blend for 1 minute. Add chicken stock and bring to a boil. Add cooked pasta, return to boil, serve immediately. Top with fresh grated Romano Cheese. BUON APPETITO!

Submitted by Michael Garozzo

GOLDEN LEAF

• Chinese Restaurant •

11839 Roe Avenue
Leawood, Kansas 66211
(913) 338-3988
Fax (913) 451-8868

Golden Leaf Chinese Restaurant specializes in Cantonese and Szechuan cuisine. It also serves some Thailand dishes. The favorite dishes are General Tso's Chicken, Red Curry Chicken and Walnut Shrimp.

Sweet & Sour Chicken

1 lb. Chicken Tenders
Marinade:

1 Dash Garlic Powder
1/4 tsp. Salt

1 Dash White Pepper
1 tsp. Wine

Batter:

2 Cups Flour
2 Eggs
1/2 Gallon Shortening

1 Cup Cornstarch
5 tbsp. Oil
2 Cups Water

Sauce:

1 tbsp. Orange Juice
1 tbsp. Pineapple Juice
3 tbsp. Sugar
1 tbsp. Ketchup.
2 Cups Water
1 Dash Salt

1 tbsp. Lemon Juice
1 tbsp. Ginger Juice
Vinegar, 2 tbsp.
1 Dash Red Food Color
1 tbsp. Corn Starch

Directions

Cut chicken tenders in 1/2-inch pieces. Marinate for 1/2 hour. Mix the batter. Dip chicken in batter, deep fry in 350 degree shortening until golden brown. Put sauce ingredients in sauce pan and make sauce.

Submitted by James Chang

GREAT PLAINS CATTLE CO.

AMERISTAR CASINO & HOTEL
Great Plains Cattle Co.
3200 North Ameristar Drive, Kansas City, MO 64161
(800) 499-4961 or (816) 414-7000

This warm, uniquely designed restaurant takes its inspiration from the frontier towns of the Great Plains - combining the rich style of a 19th century steakhouse with the rustic look of the great stockyards. The menu is certainly grand enough for a cattle baron. Among the most wanted items are Snakebites, a fried rattlesnake appetizer, colossal onion ring, buffalo rib eye and the hefty 20-ounce Bone-In Prime Rib. There's also a refined chicken with wild mushrooms and a well-chosen wine list. A private dining room may be reserved and there's a cozy, separate 72-seat lounge is warm, uniquely designed restaurant takes its inspiration from the frontier towns of the Great Plains.

Wild Boar Lolly Poops with Sweet Potato Hash

Serves 4

1 ea. Wild Boar Rack (2.5 - 3 lb. average)
2 T. Garlic (chopped)
1/2 T. Thyme (chopped)
1/4 T. Black Pepper

1/2 Cup Olive Oil
2 T. Shallots (chopped)
1/2 T. Kosher Salt

Combine oil, garlic, shallots and thyme together and allow the wild boar to marinate for at least 24 hours.

Season rack: in a large skillet on very high heat sear the racks and finish in the oven for 10-15 minutes at 375 degrees or to desired temperature. Cut into chops and arrange over the sweet potato has. Finish with a light drizzle of huckle berry gastric.

Huckle Berry Gastric

1 pt. Huckle Berries (cleaned and stemmed)
1/2 Cup Water
1/2 ea. Vanilla Bean

1/2 Cup Red Wine Vinegar
1/2 Cup Sugar
1/4 T. Kosher Salt

Combine all ingredients together and allow simmering for 30 minutes. Puree and return to heat and reduce the mixture by 1/2 or until it coats the back of a spoon.

Sweet Potato Hash

2 ea. Jumbo Sweet Potatoes (peeled, dice 1/2", and lightly blanched)

1 ea. Red Pepper (1/2" dice)
1 ea. Green Pepper (1/2" dice)
1 T. Garlic (chopped)
1/4 T. Parsley (chopped)
4 T. Butter

1 ea. Yellow Pepper (1/2" dice)
1/2 ea. Red Onion (1/2" dice)
1/4 T. Thyme (chopped)
1 T. Maple Syrup
Salt and Pepper

In a sauté skillet add the butter to melt and sauté the peppers, onion and garlic for one minute. Add the blanched sweet potatoes and sauté for 2 minutes on med-high heat to color the potatoes. Add thyme, parsley and maple syrup. Adjust seasoning with salt and pepper.

Submitted by Edward Allen, Executive Chef

HABANERO'S

1008 SE Blue Parkway
Lee's Summit, MO
(816) 554-1008

5th & Metropolitan
Leavenworth, KS
(913) 682-7300

Open every day from 11 a.m.

No time to Dine? Use our convenient
Phone-In Drive up window

Habanero's home of the flying pepper now has its second location open in Leavenworth. The Lee's Summit location on 50 highway which features an authentic yellow airplane perched on the roof will be celebrating it's ninth birthday this year. Now that same great southwest style Mexican food can be found in the north land along with a second yellow airplane proudly mounted on top of a shiny new building at 5th and Metropolitan, directly across from the entrance to the military base.

Made from scratch recipes using the finest fresh ingredients available is what makes Habanero's unique and the best in town. The 3 salsas (regular mild, crash & burn–hot, and fire fire fire–super hot) are all made fresh daily and complimentary chips are cooked up hot through the day. The long time dedicated staff at Habanero's will make you realize that a Mexican restaurant without a plane on top, just won't fly.

Habanero's Made-From-Scratch Tamales

This recipe takes several steps over 3 days.

FOR THE PORK CHILI

3 Lbs. Diced Pork, Cubed
1/8 Cup Jalapenos, Freshly Chopped
1 Tsp. Granulated Garlic Salt
1/4 Tsp. Paprika

1-1/2 Cups Plus 1/3 Cup Water, Divided
1/8 Cup White Onions, Diced
Dash of Black Pepper
3 Cups Salsa

In a large pan, cook pork in the 1-1/2 cups of water on high heat. Stir occasionally and continue to cook until pork becomes tender and most of the liquid is gone. Add jalapenos, onions and dry ingredients. Continue cooking for 5 minutes. Add salsa and 1/3 cup water. Bring to a boil and then remove from heat. Transfer to cold container and refrigerate overnight.

FOR THE TAMALE MEAT

1/2 Gallon Cold Pork Chili Meat
1/2 Tbsp. Cayenne Pepper

1/4 Cup Chili Powder

Mix all ingredients together.

FOR THE TAMALE MASA

10 oz. Lard
1/4 Tbsp. Cumin
1/4 Cup Lukewarm Water

1-1/4 Lbs. Fresh Masa
1/4 Tbsp. Baking Powder
Corn Husks

1/4 Tbsp. Granulated Garlic
2 oz. Chicken Base
5 oz. Masa-harina

Place lard in mixer. Add masa, garlic, cumin and baking powder. Mix thoroughly. Mix chicken base with water and add slowly to mixture as it mixes. Mix until masa is creamy yet firm enough to roll into balls. Place corn husks in pan and wash with hot water. Portion out 3 oz. balls of finished masa. Spread masa evenly 1/2 in. thick onto corn husk. Portion 4-oz. of pork mixture on top of masa. Fold over husk sides to cover, turn down small end of husk and leave other end open. Wrap finished tamale in waxed paper and refrigerate overnight. When ready to serve, place wrapped tamales in a perforated double boiler and steam on high for 15 minutes, then on low for 1 hour.

Submitted by Vince Totta

HANNAH BISTRO CAFÉ

**7070 W. 105th Street
(Metcalf & 105th)
Overland Park, KS 66212
(913) 383-1000**

"Hannah Bistro Café combines the variety of a bistro and the warmth of a neighborhood café. Featuring French-inspired American cuisine, Hannah offers a diverse menu, eclectic wine list and exceptional service at moderate prices. Hannah Bistro Café is a place to relax and share food, wine and conversation with someone you care about."

Roasted Diver Scallop, Celery Root and Mushroom Duxelle Lasagna with Asparagus Confit and Cumin/Carrot Broth

CELERY LASAGNA
1 Large Celery Root (cooked in 3 ups of milk)
1 Tbsp. Butter   1 oz. Cream
Put all of this in food processor and cool.
Cut cooked pasta sheet lasagna in round shape.

DUXELLE
1/2 lb. Button Mushrooms   2 Shallots
1 Garlic Clove   Salt & Pepper
Put all of this in food processor and cook for 15 minutes. Refrigerate.

MONTAGE:
LASAGNA – DUXELLE – LASAGNA – CELERY – LASAGNA

Directions

Pan-sear the scallops. Add salt/pepper and thinly slice the scallop. Fan the sliced scallops over the lasagna. Confit the asparagus in olive oil, lemon and fresh thyme. Add a teaspoon over the scallops. Juice the carrots and bring to a boil. Add olive oil and emulsify. Add a touch of cumin and pour the broth on a plate. Warm the lasagna in a 300 degree oven and set on the late. Serve! Voila!

Submitted by Chef Patrick Quillec

HEREFORD HOUSE

**** KANSAS CITY'S ORIGINAL ****

20th & Main, Kansas City, MO • (816) 842-1080
5001 Town Center Drive, Leawood, KS • (913) 327-0800
4931 W. 6th Street, Lawrence, KS • (785) 842-2333
19721 E. Jackson Dr., Independence, MO • (816) 795-9200
Zona Rosa – 8661 Stoddard, North Kansas City, MO 64153 • (816) 584-9000

Very few American steakhouses come close to the consistent excellence and quality standards that The Hereford House has mastered for nearly 48 years. Even fewer have earned the national reputation that makes this independent restaurant a favorite of legendary sports figures, Hollywood celebrities and even a few U.S. Presidents.

What's our secret? Sterling Silver Premium Beef. It comes from premium cattle bred and raised in the high plains of North America. We like to say that Hereford House beef makes life taste better.

With five locations around the metro area, you'll never find yourself too far away from this Kansas City tradition. Go ahead. Consider tonight's dinner plans made. Fire up your car and head over to one of our area restaurants. We'll fire up our grill for the best steak dinner you've ever enjoyed. See you at the Hereford House!

Shrimp Scampi

2 Lbs. Shrimp
1/4 Cup White Wine

3 Tbsp. Garlic Butter
Salt & Pepper to Taste

Directions

Place sauté pan on medium heat. Add garlic butter to pan and allow to melt at least half way. Add shrimp to pan and sauté for about 3 minutes.

Slowly pour in white wine and continue to cook until shrimp are done. Place shrimp over a steak, chicken, or simply top with breadcrumbs and brown the top.

I prefer to use 16-20 black tiger shrimp and a drinkable white wine.

Garlic Butter

1 lb. Butter (softened)
1 Tbsp. Parsley (chopped)
Lemon Juice 1/2 fresh squeezed
Pinch White Pepper

Shallots (minced) 1/2 ea.
Garlic (fresh minced) 1 Tbsp.
Pinch Salt

Directions

Combine all ingredients in the bowl of the Kitchen-Aid. Using the paddle attachment, mix on speed ONE until all ingredients are combined.

Turn to speed THREE and blend for 1 minute or until just whipped. Do not over mix.

Submitted by Hereford House

JAKE'S SMOKEHOUSE BAR & GRILL

8314 Wornall Rd.
Kansas City, MO 64114
(816) 444-1517
Fax (816) 444-5817

After 36 years at 5107 Main St., Jake Edwards Bar-B-Que has relocated farther south and changed its name to Jake's Smokehouse Bar & Grill. The new location is 8314 Wornall Rd.

"We smoke it real slow" and are still "Home of the Sweet Potato Fries."

Smoked Marinade Tenderloin

1/4 Cup Soy Sauce
1/4 Cup Worcestershire Sauce
1 lbs. Beef Tenderloin
2 Tbsp. Coarse Ground Black Pepper
1/2 Cup Water
1/2 Cup Oil, Preferred Canola or Corn

1 Tsp. White Pepper
2 Tbsp. Brown Sugar
1/2 Tsp. Ground Ginger
4 Garlic Cloves, Minced

Directions

At least four hours and up to 12 hours before you plan to barbeque, combine the marinade ingredients in a ladded jar. Place the tenderloin in a plastic bag or shallow dish and pour the marinade over the meat. Turn the meat occasionally if needed to saturate the surface with the marinade. Prepare the smoker for barbecuing, bringing the temperature to 200 degrees to 220 degrees.

Submitted by Mike Baker

JASPER'S RESTAURANT

1201 W. 103rd Street
Kansas City, MO 64114
(816) 941-6600
Fax (816) 941-4346

Jasper's, Kansas City's oldest and most authentic Italian Restaurant has been open at our new location in Watts Mill in south Kansas City for over 6 years now. For 50 years Jasper's has continued its award-winning dedication to fine Italian Cuisine and impeccable service. The menu features our famous Scampi Alla Livornese, Caesar Salad, Fresh Pastas, Veal, Steaks, and Chops as well as Fresh Seafood and Homemade Bread and Pastries. The new "Enoteca" Wine Bar features over 400 wines from Italy with many being served by the glass. The bar also features the city's largest selection of fine distilled spirits, Grappas and Espresso Coffee Drinks. Jasper and Leonard, in following with their father's legacy of dedication to fine Italian Cuisine and service have resulted in Jasper's being the most awarded restaurant in Kansas City's history.

Fettuccine Pope John XXIII

1/4 lb. Green Fettuccine
1/2 Cup Butter
1 Egg Yolk
2 Cups Cream

1/4 lb. Egg Fettuccine
1 Cup Prosciutto Ham
1/2 Cup Peas
4 Tbs. Grated Parmigiano Reggiano

Directions

In a large pot of boiling water, cook the pasta until al dente. In a large skillet, melt the butter and add the prosciutto ham. Sauté for 3-5 minutes. Add the cream and bring to a boil. Take off heat. Add the noodles, peas, egg yolk and the cheese. Toss well. Sprinkle with fresh ground black pepper.

Submitted by Jasper

JAZZ, A LOUISIANA KITCHEN

8144 NW Prairie Rd.,
Kansas City, MO
(816) 505-1714

511 SE Melody Ln.,
Lee's Summit, MO
(816) 525-9459

1823 W. 39th St.,
Kansas City, MO
(816) 531-5556

Jazz has many products we have designed to carry our own label. We have our own selection of Jazzy Merlot, White Zinfandel or Chardonnay wines, Papa Vic's Special Blended Coffee, Bon Ton Seafood Seasoning, Spicy Hot Sauce called Jazzy Voodoo Juice and our own spice Bloody Mary Mix. All items are marketed in Kansas City in a variety of grocery stores as well as sold locally in each restaurant. We also blend our own spices in bulk for use in the restaurant. We blend a meat seasoning, a seafood seasoning and a vegetable seasoning in bulk, and bottle the seafood seasoning for retail sales.

Shrimp Creole

3 1/2 lbs. Large shrimp
2 1/2 cups Basic seafood stock
5 tsp. Jazz Bon Ton Seafood Spice
5 cups Hot cooked dirty rice
1 1/2 cups Finely chopped green bell peppers

2 tsp Minced garlic
1 1/2 cups Tomato sauce
2 1/2 cups Finely chopped celery
2 1/2 Finely chopped onions, in all
4 tbsp. Unsalted butter, in all

Directions

Rinse, shell and devein shrimp. (You can make seafood stock from shells & heads)

Cook one up of the onions in a 4-qt. saucepan over high heat about 3 minutes, stirring frequently. Reduce heat to medium-low and cook, stirring frequently, until onions caramelize, 2-5 minutes. (onions should be a rich brown color, but not burned.) Add the remaining onions, the celery, bell peppers and 2 tablespoons of the butter. Cook over high heat until the bell peppers and celery start to get tender, stirring occasionally. Add garlic, and Jazz Bon Ton Seafood Spice; stir well.

Add 1/2 cup of the stock. Cook over medium heat about 5 minutes for seasonings to blend and vegetables to finish browning, stirring occasionally and scraping bottom of pan well. Add tomatoes; reduce heat to low and simmer 10 minutes, stirring occasionally and scraping pan bottom. Stir in tomato sauce and simmer 5 minutes, stirring occasionally. Add the remaining stock and sugar. Simmer 15 minutes, stirring occasionally. Add shrimp and cook just until plump and pink, 3 to 4 minutes.

Serve over dirty rice. Makes approximately 8 servings.

Submitted by Vic Allred

JAZZ, A LOUISIANA KITCHEN

8144 NW Prairie Rd.,	511 SE Melody Ln.,	1823 W. 39th St.,
Kansas City, MO	*Lee's Summit, MO*	*Kansas City, MO*
(816) 505-1714	*(816) 525-9459*	*(816) 531-5556*

In 1994 Vic Allred opened the first of four Jazz, A Louisiana Kitchen restaurants in Kansas City. Complete with wooden walls and floors, marquee lights surrounding the entire restaurant, shelves full of New Orleans and antique kitchen items, walls completely covered with New Orleans memorabilia and a menu that can only be described as authentic Cajun/Creole cuisine. One unique aspect of Jazz, A Louisiana Kitchen is its ability to attract a complete cross-section of the public. It is not unusual to see businessmen in suits completing a deal, sitting next to a young tourist couple in shorts, sitting next to an older couple toe taping to the Dixieland Jazz band. Jazz, A Louisiana Kitchen attracts every type of individual because of its value. While the food and service are first class, the price is not.

Papa Vic's Pasta

1/4 cup Sliced green onions or diced white onions
3-4 crushed garlic cloves   1/4 lb. unsalted butter or margarine
1 qt. heavy whipping cream   2 lb. Fettuccini
4 Tbsp. Jazz Bon Ton Seafood seasoning   2 lbs. ground fresh Parmesan cheese
1 1/2 cups Holy Trinity (this is traditionally green bell pepper, celery and onions, but can be any combination of your favorite veggies thinly sliced or chopped
2 lbs. boneless skinless chicken breast meat chopped into one inch pieces
1/2 cup sliced washed mushrooms

Directions

In 3 qt. sauce pan, boil 2 qts. water and cook Fettuccini al dente or until slightly undercooked. Cool under running water and set aside.

In large sauté pan, sauté chicken until coated in garlic, green onions, butter and 1 tbsp. Bon Ton Seasoning. Add 1/2 cup of water and add Holy Trinity. Reduce until chicken is cooked and remove from heat.

In 3 qt. sauce pan and under medium heat, heat heavy whipping cream and 3 tbsp. Bon Ton spices until it comes to a slow rolling boil. Stir constantly. While stirring, add Parmesan cheese and reduce until all cheese is melted.

Combine all ingredients by adding chicken and Fettuccini with the cream sauce. Continue stirring until rich and creamy. Add mushrooms last.

Service in the center of a large plate or bowl. Garnish with chopped parsley.

Yields 2-4 servings.

Submitted by Vic Allred

JERRY'S BAIT SHOP

13412 Santa Fe Trail Drive
Lenexa, KS 66215
(913) 894-WORM (9676)

811 W. 17th St.
Kansas City, MO 64108
(816) 472-1111

THE BAR & GRILL IN OLD TOWN LENEXA

Jerry's Bait Shop has been serving the Lenexa / Kansas City areas for 11 years running, offering a full menu, a wide selection of beers and great live music. "A warm shot of tequila and an ice cold beer served in a friendly, family atmosphere".

Fish Tacos with Guacamole

4 pieces fresh halibut, steak or filets, 6 to 8 ounces each
Extra-virgin olive oil, for drizzling   Salt and pepper
1 lime, juiced   1 lemon, juiced
3 small to medium ripe Haas avocados, pitted and scooped from skins with a large spoon
1/2 teaspoon cayenne pepper, eyeball it   1 cup plain yogurt
1 teaspoon coarse salt, eyeball it   2 plum tomatoes, seeded and chopped
2 scallions, thinly sliced on an angle   1 heart Romaine lettuce
12 soft (6-inch) flour tortillas

Directions

Preheat a grill pan or indoor grill to high heat or, prepare outdoor grill. Drizzle halibut with extra-virgin olive oil to keep fish from sticking to the grill pan or grill. Season fish with salt and pepper, to your taste. Roll lime on the counter top to get juices flowing. Also, any under ripe citrus may be placed in a microwave oven for 10 seconds at high setting to induce the juices to flow. Grill fish 4 to 5 minutes on each side or until opaque. Squeeze the juice of 1 lime down over the fish and remove from the grill pan or grill. Flake fish into large chunks with a fork.

While fish is cooking, in a blender or food processor, combine avocado flesh, lemon juice, cayenne pepper, yogurt and salt. Process guacamole sauce until smooth. Remove guacamole sauce to a bowl and stir in diced tomatoes and chopped scallions. Shred lettuce and reserve.

When fish comes off the grill pan or grill, blister and heat soft taco wraps. To assemble, break up fish and pile some of the meat into soft shells and slather with guacamole sauce. Top with shredded lettuce, fold tacos over and eat!

Submitted by Mike and John

KABAL RESTAURANT & NIGHTCLUB

503 Walnut
Kansas City, MO 64106
(816) 471-0017

Kabal Restaurant & Nightclub is located on the corner of 5th and Walnut in the River Market area. We are open for lunch Tuesday through Friday, 11-2 and serve dinner Tuesday through Friday 5-10, Saturday 6-10. Offering American cuisine with a Mediterranean flair. For a business-minded lunch, join us for freshly prepared soups, handcrafted salads and sandwiches with daily lunch specials. Our dinner menu features hand cut steaks, seafood and more! A full bar features domestic and imported liquors, mixed drinks, wines and beers. Happy Hour is Tuesday through Friday 5-7. Join us for half-price appetizers and drink specials.

Pasta Margherita con Gamberetto
(Pasta Margherita with Prawns)

Makes 1 serving
5-6 large prawns
2-3 lrg. fresh basil leaves
Approx. 7 oz. white wine
2 oz. uncooked fettuccine

1 med. tomato- diced
1 Tbsp. crushed garlic
1-1/2 Tbsp. cold unsalted butter

Directions

Boil water for pasta. Combine diced tomato, chopped basil and 1/2 Tbsp. of garlic in a large non-metallic bowl. Cover and let stand at least 15 minutes in refrigerator. Add pasta to boiling water. While pasta is cooking, prepare sauce. In a large saucepan, add wine and remaining garlic, cook over medium-high heat. Reduce wine by almost half. Add cold unsalted butter to sauce. As butter melts, add prawns and continue to cook, approx. 2-3 minutes or until shrimp is cooked through. Add tomato/basil mixture to sauce and simmer approx. 30 seconds. Drain pasta. Remove sauce from heat and toss with pasta.

Submitted by Robert Waterfield, Chef

KC MASTERPIECE BARBECUE & GRILL

I-435 & Metcalf
Overland Park, KS 66215
(913) 345-1199

On the Country Club Plaza
47th & Wyandotte
Kansas City, MO
(816) 531-7111

KC Masterpiece® Barbecue and Grill serves outstanding, authentic barbecue and other smoked meats in combination with original, premium side-dishes and desserts. An emphasis on authentic barbecue cooking distinguishes KC Masterpiece® Restaurants from their competition. At the restaurants all meat is grilled or smoked using 100% hickory wood. While barbecue is the featured offering, the restaurants also offer homemade soups, salads, grilled chicken, fish and premium steaks. Many of these original items like Onion Straws, Doc's Dip, KCM Baked Beans and the Chocolate Peanut Butter Ice Cream Pie have received the praise of customers and press alike for their mouth-watering flavors for over 18 years.

Barbecued Whole Tenderloin

This recipe won first prize at the Colorado Beef Growers' contest using beef tenderloin and first prize at the American Royal Barbecue Contest in 1980 using whole pork tenderloin.

1 Whole Beef Tenderloin, 4-5 lbs., Well Trimmed

Marinade & Baste
1 Cup Soy Sauce
3 Large Garlic Cloves, Minced

1/3 Cup Toasted Sesame Oil
1 Tbsp. Ground Ginger

Sauce
1 (18 oz.) Bottle KC Masterpiece BBQ Sauce
1/4 Cup Toasted Sesame Oil

1/3 Cup Soy Sauce
1 Large Garlic Clove, Finely Minced

Directions

Combine marinade ingredients and set aside 1/2 cup for basting.

Put whole tenderloin with remaining marinade in a large zip lock bag and marinate overnight in the refrigerator.

Place tenderloin on a prepared charcoal grill (with moistened hickory chips added to smoke) over a low fire, turning every 15 minutes and basting with reserved marinade.

Barbecue with lid closed until beef is done to 175-200 degrees. Use a meat thermometer to determine your choice of doneness.

Combine sauce ingredients, stir well and heat gently. Serve warm with meat.

NOTE: For indoor barbecuing, rub tenderloins generously with liquid hickory or mesquite smoke, marinate overnight in above mixture, then cook in a 300 degree preheated oven following basting direction to desired doneness.

Submitted by Rich Davis

LA COCINA DEL PUERCO

91st & Metcalf
Overland Park, KS 66212
(913) 341-2800

www.lacocinadelpuerco.com

La Cocina del Puerco has been serving Kansas City's most authentic Mexican cuisine for almost two decades. Located at the corner of 91st and Metcalf in Overland Park, this restaurant is a local tradition for fun, award winning margaritas and fantastic food. La Cocina del Puerco also features a covered patio for outside dining and live music.

"Mexican Food so authentic, you'll be afraid to drink the water."

Cochinita Pibil

Makes 24 servings
16 lbs. Pork Butt,* Chunked or Loin
1 Cup boiling Water
12 Allspice Berries (whole)
2 T. Salt
4 T. White Vinegar
Corn Tortillas, as needed
Marinate 1 Full Day Before Serving

4 T. Achiote Seed (annatto seeds)
1 T. Mexican Oregano
16 Garlic Cloves
1 Cup Fresh Seville Orange Juice
Banana Leaves, as needed

Directions

Soften banana leaves slightly over open flame. Reserve. Crush achiote lightly before putting it into blender. Add water, oregano, allspice, garlic, salt, orange juice and vinegar. Blend until smooth. Spread paste over meat, subbing well to coat all sides. Refrigerate; marinate overnight.

Place rack in bottom of large stockpot or Dutch oven, spread banana leaves on top. Add water to cover bottom of pan beneath leaves, but no higher. Transfer pork and marinade onto banana leaves, cover pan with tight-fitting lid. Cook at 400 degrees F about 2 hours. Remove from oven, turn meat, baste with drippings. Cover. Return to oven; cook until fork-tender, about 2 hours.

Strain meat, reserve drippings. Shred, then pour pan juices on top. Top with pickled onions. Serve hot with corn tortillas.

Submitted by Mike Thayer

LA MESA MEXICAN RESTAURANT

12225 Strang Line Rd.
Olathe, KS 66062
(913) 254-1999

9058B Metcalf
Overland Park, KS 66212
(913) 383-3733

110 Cunningham Pkwy.
Belton, MO 64012
(816) 331-6609

La Mesa Mexican Restaurant started as a dream of Francisco Oñate from Jalisco, Mexico. In August 1993 the first restaurant was opened in St. Joseph, Mo. It continues to be one of the best restaurants in that area.

Since then La Mesa has expanded to Kansas and Nebraska and now has 11 locations.

La Mesa Mexican Restaurant was named after the place "Rancho" where Oñate was born: "La Mesa." The success of La Mesa can be attributed to the hard work and determination of Mr. Oñate as well as other things. He never gave up on his dream and worked very hard to achieve it. The food at La Mesa is some of the best around. Everything is made fresh and service is excellent.

La Mesa may not be well known across the country (yet) but it is loved in the communities in where it is located.

Special de la Mesa

4 oz. Beef (carne azada)
2 oz. Chorizo
6 oz. Tomato
3 oz. Bell Pepper

7 oz. Chicken
10 Large Shrimps
4 oz. Onions

Directions

With our special recipe we grilled the shrimp, chicken, chorizo and carne azada to a point where it is tender and juicy, then we mix it with the vegetables for 3 minutes, allowing the meat to absorb all the vegetables flavors, creating a unique taste. Serve with rice and beans, a cheese quesadilla, sour cream, lettuce, guacamole, pico de gallo and tortillas to give it a classic Mexican look.

Submitted by Ernesto Oropeza

LUCKY BREWGRILLE

5401 Johnson Drive
Mission, KS
(913) 403-8571

www.luckybrewgrille.com

The Best Kept Secret in Mission, Kansas is at 5401 Johnson Drive in the Mission Mart Shopping Center. The Lucky Brewgrille was established in Manhattan, Kansas in the summer of 1993. The Lucky Brewgrille then moved to the Big City in January of 2001 at its present address.

Our attitude of making cooking fun and our guests welcome is the blueprint of our success. Our goal is to capture the rapture of the open sky and the open flame, to celebrate the elemental glories of grilling and the deliciously unpretentious food that forms the roots of the craft of cooking. Our focus is the foods Americans love to eat and to be creative in working directly with fire.

Join us for some hot times ahead! The Lucky Brewgrille is where smart people like to eat. FIRE UP!

Caution! Hot and Spicy Addicts Only!

Ragin Cajun Pasta

8 oz. Linguine Pasta
4 oz. Ragin Chicken
1 Tbsp. Ragin Seasoning
1 Cup Tomatoes, Diced sliced
1/4 Cup Red Peppers, 1/4x3" sliced
4 oz. Chicken Stock
2 Tbsp. White Wine, Table
1 ea. Bread Stick

1 Tbsp. Olive Oil
4 ea. Shrimp, Uncooked
1 Tbsp. Olive Oil
1/4 Cup Green Pepper, 1/4x3"

1/4 Cup White Onion, Sliced
1 Tbsp. Corn Starch
1 Tbsp. Scallions, Diced

Directions

Place linguine pasta in hot water. Cook until tender. Heat 1 tablespoon of olive oil in skillet. Add chicken and ragin seasoning. Cook until done. Add shrimp and ragin seasoning. Cook until done.

Add another 1 tablespoon of olive oil to skillet. Add tomatoes, peppers, and onion–sauté until tender. Add chicken stock and reduce. Add corn starch and white wine, stir continuously until sauce becomes thick. Add pasta and lightly toss. Serve on large plate. Top with scallions, bread stick and pasta spoon.

Submitted by Greg Fuciu

MELBEE'S BAR & RESTAURANT

6120 Johnson Drive
Mission, KS
(913) 262-6121

Mission's only fine dining restaurant is sure to please. Chef Tom Harley's progressive American menu changes seasonally and MelBee's features a new artist every six weeks. Its always new and exciting at MelBee's, so come to your new favorite place.

Walnut Crushed Chicken Breast

4 Chicken breasts
6 oz. Gorgonzola cheese crumbles
2 cups Walnuts (chopped fine)
Olive oil

3 Pears (peeled & diced)
2 medium Shallots (diced)
1 pt. Raspberries.

Directions

Preheat oven to 350 degrees. Hollow out chicken breast by inserting a knife, mix pears, cheese, shallots in medium bowl. Stuff mixture into breast incision spreading evenly. Crust with walnuts and sauté with olive oil over medium heat 3 minutes each side. Put in 350 degree oven for 10 minutes. Plate chicken topped with fresh raspberries. Enjoy.

Submitted by Tom Harley

MILANO
ITALIAN DINING

CROWN CENTER RESTAURANTS BY HYATT
Milano Italian Dining
2450 Grand Street
Kansas City, MO 64108
(816) 435-4119, Fax (816) 435-4124

Milano is an upscale Italian restaurant situated in a glass pavilion overlooking Crown Center Square. The casual environment, impeccable service, and authentic Italian cuisine combine to create a distinctive recipe for an afternoon or evening that will surpass all expectations. Experience Italy at its best. . .right in the heart of Kansas City. Need somewhere to gather after work? The newly renovated Bar at Milano is the perfect place to relax and unwind.

Milano Tortellini in a Creamy White Truffle Sauce

8 oz. Meat tortellini
1 oz. Butter
1 oz. Carrot Ribbons
1/4 oz. White Truffle Oil

4 oz. Heavy Cream
1 oz. Peas
3 oz. Diced Tomatoes
1/2 oz. Grana

Directions

Place butter and cream sauce in saute pan over medium heat. Reduce bream until it starts to thicken. Add white truffle oil, diced tomatoes, carrots, and peas. Season with salt and pepper and continue to reduce until desired thickness. Blanch tortellini in boiling water until they float. Add to cream sauce and toss with Parmesan cheese.

Submitted by Dominic Vaccaro, Executive Sous Chef, CCRH

NEIL SMITH'S COPELAND'S OF NEW ORLEANS

Neil Smith's Copeland's of New Orleans
11920 Metcalf
Overland Park, KS 66213
(913) 663-5290

Neil has stopped sacking QB's to hit our guests in the stomach with 28-day hand selected steaks, fresh fish and seafood, pastas and more. Neil has been a franchise owner for about 10 years with Copeland's and guarantees you'll love it. Neil's favorites are the Al & Jens Filet and the Hot Crab Claw appetizers. Come try them for yourself and discover a menu that will please anyone's taste buds.

Crawfish Etouffee

Serves 6

6 Cups Water	2 Bay Leaves
1 Tsp. Lobster Base	1 lb. Fresh Crawfish Tail Meat
Pinch Black Pepper	Pinch White Pepper
Pinch Cayenne	1 Tbsp. Paprika
1 oz. Peanut Oil	1 Cup Chopped Yellow Onion
4 Tsp. Flour	Salt to Taste
1 Cup Chopped Green Onions	1 Tsp. Minced Garlic
3 Tbsp. Finely Chopped Parsley	6 Cups Cooked White Rice

Directions

Prepare stock by bringing the water to a boil. Add bay leaves and lobster base. Allow to boil for about 20 minutes or until the water has reduced to 5 cups of stock. Hold aside.

In a mixing bowl, combine the crawfish tails with black, white, and cayenne pepper. Add the paprika and stir together well.

In a medium-sized pot, heat the peanut oil at a near-high setting. Oil should be hot but not smoking. Add the chopped yellow onion and stir until translucent. Add the crawfish tails and stir until they are heated and cooked through and have attained a good bond with their fat. Add flour and mix well.

Pour in stock gradually, stirring constantly, until sauce achieves a substantial thickness and consistency. Season with salt to taste.

Add the green onions, garlic and parsley. Reduce the heat to a medium setting and simmer for about 10 minutes more. Serve over a bed of cooked white rice.

Note: If desired, you may stir in 2-3 tbsp. of butter to completed etouffé for added richness.

Submitted by Nicolas Carr

OLD SHAWNEE PIZZA

61st & Nieman Rd.
Shawnee, KS 66203
(913) 631-5716
(913) 631-5737

34th & Gibbs Rd.
Kansas City, KS
(913) 677-1844

www.shawneepizza.com

In May of 1969, Joe Walker opened a pizza restaurant in Shawnee, Kansas in the old McAnany home. After more than 15 successful years at that location, he decided to move across the street to a larger location at 60th and Nieman Rd.

In 2003, after many previous years with the franchise, Joe struggled with the decision to break away and start his own franchise. This brings us to where we are today. The previous franchise, and Old Shawnee Pizza, have been run by Joe and his family for more than 35 years which makes it the oldest operating restaurant in Shawnee.

Hours are Sunday through Thursday from 11 a.m. to 9 p.m. and Friday and Saturday from 11 a.m. to 10 p.m.

We offer classic pizzas, pastas, sandwiches and salads as well as specialty items such as the Mama Mia, an alfredo pizza offered with either chicken or shrimp and our new Grilled Vegetable Lasagna.

We were recently voted in the top three for Best Lunch and Best Pizza in the "Best of Shawnee 2005." You can find all the information about Old Shawnee Pizza, as well as print coupons, by visiting our website at www.shawneepizza.com

Mom's Homemade Lasagna

1/2 lb. ground beef
1 16 oz. can tomato sauce
1 lb. mozzarella cheese
1 box lasagna noodles

1/2 lb. ground Italian sausage
1 pkg. spaghetti sauce seasoning
1 pt. cottage cheese
1 c. parmesan cheese

Directions

In 9x9 inch pan layer browned meat mixed with tomato sauce and seasoning, noodles, cottage cheese, parmesan and mozzarella. Keep adding layers until full, ending with mozzarella. Bake in oven at 375 degrees for 45 minutes until hot in center.

Submitted by Will Walker

Paulo & Bill's

16501 Midland Dr.
Shawnee, KS 66217
(913) 962-9900
Fax (913) 962-9733

Paulo and Bill Restaurant has all the charm of a neighborhood restaurant; but combined with our friendly, professional service and excellent food; our guests know that we are truly something special. Our menu includes classic Italian food such as Lasagna, Chicken Marsala and Veal Parmesan, and then we add dishes like our Pecan Crusted Salmon, Mama Mia Tenderloin and even a KC Strip for good measure! Desserts are a must. They are all made fresh, in house, and are a perfect ending to any meal at Paulo and Bill. Reservations are encouraged.

Visit our website: pauloandbill.com for our upcoming events and complete menu listings.

Pecan Crusted Canadian Salmon

1 7 oz. Salmon Filet	3/4 Cup Wild Rice Pilaf
1/2 Cup Orange Juice	1-1/2 Qt. Chicken Stock
4 oz. Butter	1/4 Cup garlic
1/4 Cup Diced Onion	1 Tsp. Salt
1 Tsp. Black Pepper	3/4 Braised Carrots and Leeks
1/2 Cup Butter	2 oz. Chardonnay Orange Burre Blanc
1 Cup Chardonnay	1 Qt. Heavy Cream
	1/2 lb. Butter

Directions

Coat salmon fillet with soft butter and crushed pecans and bake in 350 degree oven for 8-10 minutes. Bring stock, butter, onions, garlic, salt and pepper to a boil, pour over wild rice blend. Cover and bake in oven for 35 minutes. Cut carrots and leek and braise in butter until tender. Reduce Chardonnay and orange juice 3/4, add heavy cream, reduce by 1/2, whisk in cubed cold butter finish sauce.

Submitted by Dan Drake, Executive Chef

PEARL'S OYSTER BAR

AMERISTAR CASINO & HOTEL
Pearl's Oyster Bar
3200 North Ameristar Drive
Kansas City, MO 64161
(800) 499-4961 or (816) 414-7000

The best of New Orleans comes to Kansas City. This warm, inviting restaurant takes inspiration from Creole and Cajun culture and cuisine with fresh seafood as the main attraction. You'll want to try one of their signature pan-roasts or roasted shrimp. Don't go away without sampling a slice of pecan pie.

Pearl's Pan Roast

Yield one serving
6 oz. Seafood (use shrimp, crab, mussels, oysters or any combination of these)
6 oz. Trinity (diced celery, onions, and bell peppers)
1 Tsp. Chopped Garlic   2 oz. Heavy Cream
4 oz. Pan Roast Base (see recipe)   1 Tsp. Chopped Parsley
1 Tsp. Everything Spice (see recipe) 1 Tsp. Butter
4 oz. Cooked Rice

In sauté pan, melt butter with garlic, add seafood and everything spice, sauté until nearly done. Add trinity and continue to sauté until vegetables are tender. Deglaze pan with clam juice.

Add Pan Roast Base and heavy cream. Bring to boil and add parsley, adjust seasoning if necessary.

To serve: Place Pan Roast in bowl, top with scoop of rice. Enjoy!

Pan Roast Base Stock:
1 qt. Tomato Juice   1 Qt. Claim Juice
1 Cup Worcestershire   2 oz. Unsalted Butter
2 oz. Minced Garlic   1 Cup White Wine

Melt butter and bloom garlic. Deglaze with wine, add Worcestershire, reduce by half. Add tomato and clam juice, bring to boil. Simmer 20 min. Remove from heat and chill until ready to use.

Everything Seasoning:
8 oz. Paprika   4 oz. Salt
2 oz. Thyme   2 oz. Oregano
1 oz. Cayenne Pepper   1 oz. Black Pepper
1 oz. Cumin

Blend all ingredients together.

Submitted by Edward Allen, Executive Chef

The Peppercorn Duck Club

CROWN CENTER RESTAURANTS
BY HYATT
The Peppercorn Duck Club
2345 McGee Street
Kansas City, MO 64108
(816) 435-4199, Fax (816) 421-1550

The Peppercorn Duck Club is a 25-year Kansas City tradition and Hyatt Regency Crown Center's fine dining restaurant. Centrally located in Kansas City, it is the perfect place for business lunches, special occasions, or a night on the town. Decorated in rich colors of brocade and brass, The Peppercorn Duck Club has a setting appropriate for the service and quality known to its guests. The Specialty of the house is the ever popular rotisserie duckling. And for guests who appreciate chocolate, the Peppercorn Duck Club offers the Ultra Chocolatta dessert bar, a selection of rich chocolate desserts prepared by the pastry chef. The Ultra Chocolatta Bar is offered complimentary for lunch and dinner with the purchase of an entrée.

Chicken St. Topaz

1 (7 oz.) Chicken Breast
2 Shrimp
1/4 Cup Crab Meat
2-3 oz. Sweet Potato Puree
1/4 lb. Butter
Salt & Pepper to Taste
Shallots (Julienne) 1/2 shallot
1 Cup Heavy Cream

2 Scallops
1/4 Cup Clam Meat
2 oz. Bechamel Chardonnay Cream Sauce
Vegetables Choice
Flour as needed
1 qt. Chicken Base
1 clove French Garlic (chopped)

Directions

Melt butter over medium heat in skillet. Lightly flour chicken breast and sauté chicken until golden brown on both sides. Remove chicken and set aside. In same skillet, sauté scallops for 2 min. Add shrimp and sauté for 1 more minute. Add garlic and shallots continue to sauté for 1-2 minutes. Add cream and lower heat and reduce to desired thickness. Slowly stir in remaining butter to incorporate into cream. Add chicken base and keep stirring. Add salt and pepper to taste. Add chicken and let simmer for another minute. Place chicken on plate with shrimp and scallops on top of chicken and pour sauce around the plate.

Chef Suggestion for Vegetables: Asparagus, baby carrots with tops.

Submitted by Giovanni D'Angelo, Sous Chef

PICKERING'S PUB & EATERY

Pickering's
Pub & Eatery

11922 Strang Line Road
Olathe, KS 66062
(913) 782-6464 • Fax (913) 782-5399

When Pickering's Pub and Restaurant opened on Sept. 9, 1994, it was the first sports bar on the corner of 119th and Strang Line Road. Since then, the growth has been unbelievable.

Pickering's is owned by Olathe locals Paul and Patty Boone, both of whom grew up in the restaurant business. Paul and Patty take pride in their high standards of quality food and friendly service. As a matter of fact, they have established quite a reputation for excellent food and a very comfortable atmosphere. These high standards are apparent when you dine at Pickering's. Local favorites range from their homemade honey mustard salad dressing to their giant tenderloin sandwich or a hand cut K.C. Strip.

Vegetable Kabobs

We grill meat and vegetables on separate skewers to keep from overcooking the vegetables.

1 Green, Yellow & Red Bell Pepper   1 Onion
1 Container Button Mushrooms   1 Container Grape Tomatoes
1 Yellow or Green Zucchini

Cut vegetables into 1" chunks. Carefully place on bamboo or metal skewer rotating the vegetable order. Marinate in Italian salad dressing for 45 minutes. Grill until done.

Chicken Kabobs

1 Package Boneless, Skinless Chicken Breast

Cut chicken breast into strips or chunks. Carefully place on bamboo or metal skewer. Marinate for one hour.

Chicken Marinade

1/4 Cup Heinz 57 Steak Sauce   1/4 Cup Honey   1/2 Cup Worcestershire

Submitted by Paul & Patty Boone

PIZANO'S ITALIAN CAFE

13316 Metcalf Ave.
Overland Park, KS 66213
(913) 681-1300

At Pizano's we hope your experience is enjoyable and satisfying! We are a local family owned and operated business and realize our desires and future success is predicated on establishing happy and satisfied guests who repeatedly dine at our establishment.

We also provide a specialized and trained staff in catering and delivery services. We also offer a semi-private room in-house that can accommodate up to 40 guests. Please consider us for any and all of your special event needs or office luncheons. Pizano's "Good Friends"...Great Food!

Angel Hair D'Mare

Angel Hair Pasta, 2 lbs.
1/4 cup good quality olive oil
1 cup fresh basil, chopped
8 medium to large scallops
8-12 fresh clams w/shells (optional)
1-2 tsp. black pepper or to taste
1 tsp. crushed red pepper or to taste

White wine 2 cups
4 cups chicken stock
16 medium to large shrimp
1 6 oz. can chopped clams w/juice
1 14 oz. can crushed or diced tomato
  w/juice
1 tsp salt

Directions

Combine olive oil and garlic in a wide narrow pot or large skillet. Cook at medium heat until garlic becomes soft and slightly golden, then add white wine, chicken stock, claim juice, black pepper, red pepper and salt. Let simmer for 5 minutes. (This can be done in advance)

Cook pasta in boiling water until firm, remove and strain. (Angel hair pasta cooks faster than regular pasta)

Add shrimp, scallops and tomatoes with juice to sauce, cook at high temp for five minutes, discard any clam shells that did not open. Mix in fresh basil. Portion pasta in individual bowls or one large serving bowl and top with seafood and sauce. Serves 4.

Submitted by Anthony Pernice

ROMANELLI GRILL & BAR

7122 Wornall Road
Kansas City, MO
(816) 333-1321

Where Good Friends Meet

A former A&P grocery store, the Romanelli Grill & Bar has been a fixture in Brookside, MO since 1935. The present owner, Joe MacCabe Jr., makes it his goal to keep Romanelli's a place where neighborhood folks can meet and eat good food. Once you enter this local favorite you discover the secret to their time-honored traditions and loyal patronage: Home-style cooking and service with a smile and then some. Eat here a couple of times, and they'll know your usual order

Ham, Chicken and Sausage Jambalaya

2 lb. Chicken, Cut in Chunks
1 lb. Smoked Ham, Cut in Chunks
1 lb. Cajun Sausage (andouilli)
1-1/2 Cup Celery, Chopped
1-1/2 Cup Onion, Chopped
1/2 Stick Unsalted Butter
1/2 Tsp. Bay Leaf
1 Tsp. Garlic Powder
1/4 Tsp. White Pepper

1/4 Tsp. Red Pepper
1/4 Tsp. Black Pepper
1/4 Tsp. Thyme
1-1/2 Cup Green Pepper, Chopped
1 Cup Tomato Sauce
2 Cups Uncooked Rice
2 Cans Chicken Soup
1 Can Cream of Chicken Soup

Directions

In a bowl, combine seasonings; set aside. In a saucepan, melt butter at 450 degrees. Add chicken, ham, sausage and 1/2 seasoning mix; sauté until brown. Remove from pan and allow drippings to remain. Return pan to heat at 250 degrees. Add vegetables and sauté until light brown. Add remaining seasonings; blend well. Keep this dish constantly moving. Add tomato sauce and bring to a simmer. Return meats to pan and sauté for another 10 minutes. Add soups and any remaining ingredients except for rice. Bring to a boil. Add rice and bring to a simmer. Cook until rice is tender, but not mushy. Serve. Serves 8.

Submitted by Joe MacCabe Jr.

SKIES RESTAURANT

CROWN CENTER RESTAURANTS BY HYATT
Skies Restaurant
2345 McGee Street, 42nd Floor of Hyatt regency Crown Center
Kansas City, MO 64108
(816) 435-4199, Fax (816) 421-1550

Tired of going out to dinner at the same old restaurant? Try dinner with a TWIST in Skies, Kansas City's only revolving rooftop restaurant. Located atop the Hyatt Regency Crown Center, Skies offers spectacular panoramic view of the city paired with exquisite cuisine and creative cocktails.

The menu at Skies features generous portions of steaks and seafood grilled to perfection over applewood chips. Skies also offers an array of desserts and is famed for its Skie High Pie with layers of ice cream, a graham cracker crust, and topped with whipped cream. A KC tradition!

Blackened KC Strip with Blue Cheese & Tiger Shrimp

14 oz. KC Strip
3 oz. Gorgonzola Crumbles
2 oz. Clarified Butter

4 Shrimp (3 oz.) Cooked, Peeled, and Deveined
2 oz. Cajun Seasoning

Directions

Preheat oven to 375 degrees. Preheat cast iron skillet over high heat. Roll steak in Cajun seasoning. Add butter to skillet and place steak on top of butter. Blacken steak on both sides and remove from skillet. In baking pan, place steak, blue cheese on top of steak, then layer 4 pieces of shrimp above cheese. Bake in oven until internal temp is 130-135 degrees. If you want steak to be medium rare, cook until 125 degrees. When steak is done cooking is should still be juicy. The Gorgonzola cheese and shrimp crust should be barely bubbling and golden brown. Serve with your favorite potato and vegetables.

Submitted by Adam Clay, Sous Chef

TASSO'S GREEK RESTAURANT

**8411 Wornall Road
Kansas City, MO
(816) 363-4776
Fax (816) 363-8276**

GREEK RESTAURANT
Est. 1976

We Cater For All Occasions!

To make good, fresh food and serve it hot with a generous side order of fun. That philosophy has helped Tasso's become one of Kansas City's favorite restaurants. Tasso insists that everyone at Tasso's have a good time, including himself.

To many Kansas Citians, the name of this Greek restaurant conjures up images of Bouzouki music, belly dancing and festive plate breaking. There's plenty of all that on the weekends, but here's a lesser-known fact: During the week Tasso's is a regular place where you can enjoy tasty Greek and American food in a subdued atmosphere.

Kotopoulo Lemonato (Baked Chicken/Greek Style)

Chicken in lemon sauce

4 tbsp. olive oil
1 tsp. chopped parsley
1 cup lemon juice
1 chicken, cut into pieces

2 tbsp. white wine
1 tsp. oregano
Salt & pepper to taste

Directions

Combine all ingredients except chicken to form marinade. Refrigerate for one hour. Place chicken pieces on a flat pan, skin side down. Broil 15 minutes. Flip pieces. Brush generously with marinade and broil additional 20 minutes. Serves 4 people.

Submitted by Tasso and John Kalliris

TATSU'S FRENCH RESTAURANT

4603 W. 96th Street
Prairie Village, KS 66208
(913) 383-9801
Fax (913) 383-1770
www.tatsus.com

Tatsu's French Restaurant has been pleasing patrons for more than 20 years, providing elegant and masterful interpretations of French cuisine in a relaxed and intimate setting. French classics such as Beef Bourguignon, Saumon Poché/Meuniére and delicious Puréed Carrot Soup grace the menu. The quality of the cuisine, affordability and attentive service has created a loyal following of patrons who dine regularly at Tatsu's.

Poulet aux Herbes (Chicken with Herbs)

1 Chicken Breast
3/4 Tbsp. Thyme
3/4 Tbsp. Black Pepper
1 tsp. Chives
Dash Rosemary
3/4 Tbsp. Soy Sauce

1/4 c. Sugar
3/4 Tbsp. Oregano
3/4 Tbsp. Sesame Seeds
1 oz. Garlic
1 oz. White Wine
Dash Lemon Juice

Directions

Slice chicken in half horizontally. Mix all ingredients except for soy sauce, lemon and white wine. Sauté chicken breast in oil then add a little butter to brown. Add ingredients then white wine, lemon and soy sauce.

Submitted by Tatsu Arai

TALK OF THE TOWN

11922 W. 119th St.
Overland Park, KS 66213
(913) 661-9922
Fax (913) 661-9944

Talk of the Town – home of the best beer prices in town. A cozy bar and grill in south Overland Park, known for great service and great burgers. An adult as well as a tremendously kid-friendly bar. Talk of the Town offers specials every day. Taco Tuesday–5 tacos for 5 bucks. Half Price Burgers every Wednesday.

Rigs's Lasagna

1-1/2 lb. Ground Beef
4 Cloves Garlic
2 Large Diced Tomatoes
1 6 oz. Can Tomato Paste
2 Tbsp. Oregano
1 Egg
1 bag, Parmesan, Shredded

1 Bag Shredded Mozzarella
1 Can Diced Tomatoes
1 8 oz. Can Tomato Sauce
2 Tbsp. Basil
8 Lasagna Noodles
2-1/2 Cups Cottage Cheese

Directions

For sauce, brown meat, drain fat. Then add garlic minced, stir in tomato sauce, diced tomatoes, tomato paste, salt, pepper, basil and oregano. Bring to a boil, stirring, reduce heat and simmer for one hour, stirring occasionally.

Boil noodles for 10-12 minutes. Rinse well with cold water and drain.

For filling combine 1 egg, cottage cheese and Parmesan in separate bowl. Layer 4 noodles on a casserole dish, spread filling on them and then half sauce, then top with mozzarella, repeat one more time. Preheat oven to 375 degrees. Cover lasagna with tin foil and place in oven. Cook 30-35 minutes. Let stand 10 minutes and top with Parmesan cheese. Serves about six people.

Submitted by Brian Rigsby

THE MAJESTIC STEAKHOUSE

931 Broadway
Kansas City, MO 64105
(816) 471-8484
Fax (816) 471-7906

The restaurant takes its name from a former Kansas City Landmark, the Majestic Steakhouse, a highly popular restaurant for more than 30 years at 31st and Holmes. The new Majestic is in the restored turn-of-the-century Garment District Building that formerly housed Fitzpatrick's and the Fountain City Dining Room. The decor remains one of the city's finest, handsomely restored restaurant settings with dark old wood, a high stamped tin ceiling and leaded glass light fixtures.

Steaks are the focus of the entrée menu with both filet mignon and prime Kansas City Strip cuts available in 3 sizes. Roast Prime Rib is sold by the thickness of the cut. Grilled Salmon fillet highlights the non-beef dishes, but is followed by Fettuccine Alfredo with grilled chicken or the Fresh Fish Daily feature.

Full service bar includes a fairly priced wine list with outstanding selection (many hidden gems!) Live Jazz is played nightly.

Steak Majestic

8 oz. cut beef fillet
2 oz. Worcestershire
3 oz. green peppercorn - in brine
1/2 oz. white peppercorn
1/2 cup Brandy

1 cup heavy whipping
2 T. butter
1 1/2 oz. cracked black pepper
1/4 oz. pink peppercorn

Directions

The first step is to get a sauté skillet very hot on the stove. Place 2 Tbsp. butter (softened) in the skillet and sauté each side of the steak for 3 minutes. Remove steak from pan and deglaze the skillet with the Brandy. Put skillet on flame and let Brandy burn off for a few seconds. Next add Worcestershire and all of the peppercorns. Let this mixture reduce by one-half then add heavy cream. Place steak back into skillet and cool until sauce reaches a nice consistency.

Submitted by Chef Nelson

THE WOODLANDS KENNEL CLUB

the
WOODLANDS

Kansas City, Kansas

9700 Leavenworth Road
Kansas City, KS 66109
(913) 299-9797
Fax (913) 299-9804
www.woodlandskc.com

Set amid the gently rolling hills of Western Wyandotte County, The Woodlands is Kansas City's hottest entertainment value featuring year-round LIVE greyhound racing, fine dining in the Kennel Club, simulcast racing action and LIVE horse racing in the Fall.

The Woodlands Kennel Club Restaurant is a perfect place to relax with your favorite cocktail and enjoy some of the area's finest cuisine while witnessing all the excitement of live greyhound racing and televised sports in America. Be prepared for a dining experience with distinction and action...nonstop!

The Woodlands is located just a few blocks east of I-435 at 9700 Leavenworth Road in Kansas City, Kansas. (913) 299-9797. www.woodlandskc.com

Tri Color Tortellini and Chicken

3 oz. chicken (grilled)
1 oz. peas
2 oz. tortellini
2 oz. Parmesan cheese

1 oz. mushrooms
6 oz. garlic cream sauce
2 pieces garlic bread

Directions

Sauté onions, garlic and mushrooms, add heavy cream sauce and Parmesan cheese for 4 minutes. After that add peas and Tri Color Tortellini. Pasta served in a pasta bowl, add parsley around the plate for presentation.

Submitted by Chef Jose Nava

W.J. McBRIDE'S IRISH PUB

1340 Village West Parkway
Kansas City, KS 66111
(913) 788-7771
Fax (913) 788-2111

If you're looking for a *grand* time out with great food, drinks, service and atmosphere... look no further! W.J. McBride's Irish Pub & Restaurant fills the bill every time. Located in Village West at the Kansas Speedway (across from Cabela's & the Great Wolf Lodge), McBride's is just minutes from downtown Kansas City, Missouri; KCI Airport and suburban Johnson County, Kansas. McBride's is the home of genuine Irish hospitality and great upscale Irish pub food. This recipe is an example of our original Irish inspired cuisine. So, join us for the perfect pint of Guinness or a rare 'auld Irish whiskey and a great meal...and you'll see why W.J. McBride's has become the Emerald of Kansas City. *Slainte!* ("Good health to you!")

Irish Cheddar & Rasher Stuffed Chicken
w/Colcannon and Whiskey Mushroom Sauce

7 oz. - 4 each Chicken breast, pounded lightly
4 (1 oz . slices) Dubliner Irish Cheddar Cheese

(1 oz. slices) Rashers Irish Bacon
Salt & Pepper As Needed

3 lb. Potatoes, Idaho
2 oz. Milk
1 stalk Green onion, sliced greens only,

2 oz. Butter
Salt & Black Pepper to Taste

1 small head Green cabbage, peeled, cored and cut batonnet
1 cup Chicken stock or broth
1/4 tsp. Garlic, fresh minced

Salt & Black Pepper, pinch each
2 oz. Butter

1 lb. White mushrooms
Salt & Black Pepper, pinch each
1 T Butter

1/8 tsp. Garlic, fresh minced
1 oz. Irish Whiskey
1/4 tsp. Thyme, fresh

Directions

1. Pound chicken breast and lay 2 rashers on either breast, lay cheese and then roll tightly width wise in plastic wrap, refrigerate for 15-20 minutes

2. Peel and boil potatoes until fork tender, drain water and add ingredients for champ mash well and reserve warm for later.

3. Prep cabbage, heat soup pot over medium-high heat and melt butter, sauté garlic for 1-2 minutes then add cabbage, salt and pepper stir to combine, add chicken stock cover with lid and simmer for 15 minutes until tender.

4. Mash cabbage with champ potatoes to make colcannon and keep warm for service.

5. Heat 2oz butter and 2oz oil in sauté pan over medium-high heat brown chicken breasts in pan on all sides and place into a 350F oven for 15 minutes or until internal temperature registers 165F

6. Take chicken out of pan and drain off any grease and let rest.

7. In the same pan melt butter and sauté garlic and mushrooms for 3 minutes, add whiskey and scrape bottom of pan, bring to a boil and season with salt and pepper and the fresh thyme.

8. Scoop colcannon onto the middle of a plate and slice each chicken breast and layer them around colcannon, then spoon sauce over chicken and serve.

Submitted by Michael Cosman, C.C.C., Executive Chef

RESTAURANT Recipes of

MISCELLANEOUS

2 GUYS CHEESESTEAKS, GYROS & MORE

7201 Johnson Drive
Mission, KS
(913) 262-2155

The 2 Guys menu is written on a board. Ordering takes place at a counter. Drinks (soft drinks and iced tea) are self-serve. And food is served on disposables.

And there really are two guys: father and son Bill and Barry Cowden, who not coincidentally own Don Chilito's next door.

The food matches the décor: simple, short and guy-like with cheese steaks, gyros, salads, sandwiches, fresh-made potato chips and fries.

The cheapest sandwich on the menu is the #5; a plain cheesesteak with your choice of one vegetable ($4.99). The most expensive things are $5.95–gyro and cheese steak salads, for example. For an extra 30 cents, spring for the lunch special: half a sandwich, half salad and a drink.

2 Guys Tzatziki Sauce
(cucumber sauce)

2 Cups Sour Cream
1/2 Tsp. Dillweed
1 Tsp. White Pepper
1 Tsp. White Vinegar

1 Cup Cucumber (1 large, seeded, w/peel on)
1/4 Tsp. Garlic Powder
1/2 Tsp. Salt
2 Tsp. Olive Oil

Directions

Mince cucumber in food processor. Add sour cream and mix. Add remaining ingredients and whip together. Refrigerate, serve cold. Yields approx. 3-1/2 cups.

Submitted by Bill Cowden

11924 W. 119th Street
Overland Park, KS 66213
(913) 663-4099
Fax (913) 663-4104

16649 Midland Drive
Shawnee, KS 66217
(913) 268-5160
Fax (913) 268-5175

**BREWHAUS
& RESTAURANT**

Barley's Brewhaus offers 99 taps of beer from across the country and around the world. We also offer a wonderful made from scratch menu. We make all of our soups, sauces, salad dressings in house. We hand-cut our steaks and fresh fish daily. We even make our own sausages. Come by on game day and watch the big screen. Check us out!

Caesar Dressing

24 oz. Mayonnaise
1 T. Anchovies
1 oz. Lemon juice
1 T. Brown sugar
1 Tsp. White pepper

1 oz. Fresh chopped garlic
2.5 oz. Fresh Parmesan
1 T. Red Wine Vinegar
1 Tsp. Kosher salt

Directions

Place anchovies, garlic and vinegar in food processor and puree.
Mix all ingredients together; mix very well to distribute all the anchovies.

Submitted by KC Hopps, Ltd.

THE BLUE MOOSE BAR & GRILL

4160 W. 71st Street
Prairie Village, KS 66208
(913) 722-WINE (9463)
Fax (913) 722-9420

Blue Moose, located in the heart of Prairie Village, is a great place for lunch, dinner, happy hour or even late night. We serve a made from scratch menu in a warm and friendly atmosphere. We have 2 patios for outdoor dining and TV's for game viewing, something for everyone.

Creamy Whipped Cauliflower

3 Heads of Cauliflower1
12 oz. Cream Cheese
4 oz. Butter

Tsp. White Pepper
1 Tsp. Kosher Salt

Directions

Place cauliflower florets in boiling water.

Cook cauliflower until completely done, drain water.

Place cauliflower in mixing bowl, add cream cheese, butter, pepper and salt, mix thoroughly and serve hot.

Submitted by KC Hopps, Ltd.

CALIFORNOS WESTPORT

★ ★ ★ ★

CALIFORNOS
W E S T P O R T

4124 Pennsylvania
Kansas City, MO 64111
(816) 531-7878
Fax: (816) 531-1894

Tucked away within a picturesque cul-de-sac in the heart of Kansas City's entertainment district, Californos Westport recreates the very feel of a French bistro, complete with dark wooden bar and interior, and intimate tables covered with white tablecloths. In addition to a breezy deck out back, where friends and family dine and socialize, a wrought-iron railing encloses streetside seating out front, reminiscent of a romantic Parisian eatery. The menu offers an intriguing blend of contemporary American cuisine and European fare. You'll find the wait staff attentive and efficient, ready to satisfy all your wants and wishes.

Hazelnut Vinaigrette Dressing

4 c. salad oil
1/2 c. sugar
1/8 c. finely chopped hazelnuts

2 c. white wine vinegar
1/2 tsp. salt

Directions

Combine. Keeps for a while. Be sure to mix immediately before serving (it tends to separate a bit).

Submitted by Randy Childers

CASA PALOMA MEXICAN MARKET

8220 Metcalf Ave.
Overland Park, KS
(913) 385-9044

Tienda Casa Paloma, formerly located in Historic Union Station, moves to Overland Park! The new space allows us to be open at night and on weekends, serving our famous breakfast, lunch and dinner, all day, every day, Tuesday through Sunday from 10 a.m. to 9 p.m. We are closed on Mondays.

The recipes are all made from scratch, Veracruz style. We serve black beans, corn tortillas and tamales wrapped in banana leaves! There is a salsa bar with four different fresh produce salsas prepared daily.

Pico de Gallo

A chunky salsa great on grill steak tacos. Also wonderful topper for nachos and taco salads.

10-12 roma tomatoes
2 limes
2 fresh jalapenos

One-half yellow onion
One-half bunch fresh cilantro

Directions

Dice the tomatoes and onion. Stir until the mixture is equally distributed. Finely chop up the jalapenos (be sure to use gloves or wash your hands immediately after you handle the peppers). Add to the tomato and onion mixture.

Squeeze on the juice of both limes.

Chop the cilantro, be careful not to use the stems, and add to the mixture.

That's it.

Submitted by Lisa Lara

EVERETT'S

4835 Lake Wood Way
Lee's Summit, MO
(816) 795-5553

Everett's was started in the fall of 1987 in Columbia, MO. After 12 years the owner expanded to the Kansas City market when he opened a second store in Lee's Summit, Mo. Specializing in certified Angus beef, the locally owned restaurant has a varied menu including seafood, chicken, and pasta that is sure to meet anyone's taste. Everett's–where good times, good food, and good friends all come together.

Honey Dijon Dressing

.3 Gal Mayonnaise, Whole Egg
3.2 oz. Mustard, Dijon

1/2 lb. Sour Cream
1 lb. Honey

Directions

Place all ingredients in mixing bowl. Mix thoroughly until well blended. Place in container. Cover, label and date and place in refrigerator until needed.

Submitted by Chris Cope

FALCON DINER

AMERISTAR CASINO & HOTEL
Falcon Diner
3200 North Ameristar Drive
Kansas City, MO 64161
(800) 499-4961 or (816) 414-7000

The Falcon Diner recreates the American diner with comfortable booths, a soda fountain, and Art Deco architecture drawn from the modernist movement. The setting is typical of a downtown eatery and the menu is an American classic. Go for the cheeseburger, the Falcon Meat Loaf, or the diner's dynamite Smokehouse Chicken. Here's another great tip: try one of their incredible milkshakes. The diner serves down-home breakfasts and traditional lunch and dinner choices from early in the morning until late at night. There's also a bakery counter where you can purchase fresh-baked breads, pies and pastries to go or order a specialty coffee to start your day.

Falcon Diner Monte Cristo Sandwich

Serves 1
2 Slices Sourdough Bread
4 oz. Sliced Ham
1 Slice Swiss Cheese
2 oz. Current Jelly Sauce
Monte Cristo Batter:
1/2 Qt. Water
1 Tsp. Salt
3/4 oz. Baking Powder
Current Jelly Sauce:
10 oz. Current Jelly
1 oz. Heavy Cream

4 oz. Sliced Turkey
1 Slice American Cheese
4 oz. Monte Cristo Batter
1 Tsp. Powdered Sugar

4 Whole Eggs
9 oz. AP Flour

1 oz. Water

Directions

Prepare the batter by combining all ingredients. Prepare the current jelly spread by combining all ingredients.

Build sandwich then cut in half, secure with toothpicks, dip in batter and drain off excess, deep fry at 350 degrees until golden brown. Sprinkle with powdered sugar and serve with jelly sauce.

Submitted by Edward Allen, Executive Chef

ILIKI CAFE & WINE BAR

ILIKI café and Wine Bar

6431 N. Crosby Ave.
Kansas City, MO 64151
(816) 587-0009
Fax (816) 587-6011

Iliki Cafe & Wine Bar was founded in 1995. We feature a core menu of Mediterranean - Falafel, Humus and Kabobs for example. We also have an extensive "specials" menu that has a "world" touch. We have steaks, pastas, pizzas, Asian, French and so much more to try. This way our guests can be sure they always find something to interest them as well as satisfy. Iliki also boasts a world of wines and beers. So you can travel the world with your drinks. Recognized by Wine Spectator since 1997 as a world renowned "wines by the glass list," as many as 90 by the glass.

Loubya (Sauteéd Green Beans and Garlic)

1 1/2 Cup Green Beans
1/2 Cup Diced Tomato
1 Cup Cooked Basmati Rice

1/2 Cup Diced Onion
Tbsp. Minced Garlic

Directions

Begin by sauteéing the onion over medium high heat until translucent. (about 2 minutes) Then add the green beans, garlic and tomato. Reduce heat to medium, continue cooking for approx. 2 minutes more. Add salt and pepper to taste. Pour on a bed of Basmati rice and garnish with lemon.

Submitted by Christian Fuller

JERSEY BOYZ DELI

15102 Travis
Overland Park, KS 66085
(913) 897-7272
Fax (913) 897-0501

Mon.-Sat. 10-8
Sun. 11-5
Catering Available

Jersey Boyz, Overland Park, was originated in August 1988 by a family from New Jersey. Still owned by one of the family members, Barbara Bair, we pride ourselves on authentic Jersey style sandwiches and Philly Cheese Steaks. Jersey Boyz has a fun and friendly atmosphere.

Grilled Reuben Sandwich

Rye bread
2 slices Swiss cheese
Thousand Island dressing

4 oz. corned beef
Sauerkraut
Butter

Directions

Butter rye and grill both slices. Grill 4 oz. corned beef. When heated well add Swiss. Put on bread. Remove from grill, add kraut mixture. Put top on sandwich.

*Mix sauerkraut and Thousand Island dressing well before grilling.

Submitted by Barbara Bair

JOHNNY'S TAVERN

119th & Glenwood
Overland Park, KS
(913) 451-4542

61st Terr. & Pflumm
Shawnee, KS
(913) 962-5777

83rd & Mission Rd.
Prairie Village, KS
(913) 901-0322

135th & Quivira
Overland Park, KS
(913) 851-5165

Johnny's Tavern first opened as a neighborhood bar in Lawrence, Kansas in 1953. It has been operated under its current owner since 1978. Johnny's moved to 119th and Glenwood in Overland Park in 1991. Since the, Johnny's has opened three more locations in Johnson County–Shawnee, Prairie Village and a smoke-free location in Overland Park. Johnny's is famous for its hamburgers, but offers a wide variety of menu options. Come on in to meet new friends and have a cold one.

Johnny's Tavern Famous Dill Dip

32 oz. Mayonnaise
5 Tsp. Dried Onion
2 Tsp. Dill Weed
1/2 Tsp. Seasoning Salt

16 oz. Sour Cream
5 Tsp. Parsley Flakes
1/2 Tsp. White Pepper

Directions

Mix everything together in a large bowl. Best if made the day before.

Johnny's Tavern House Made Bleu Cheese Dressing

32 oz. Mayonnaise
10 oz. Bleu Cheese Crumble
1/2 Tsp. Tabasco
1/2 Tsp. Garlic Powder

20 oz. Sour Cream
2 Tsp. Lea & Perrins
1/2 Tsp. Seasoning Salt
Juice from 1/2 Lemon

Directions

Mix everything together in a large bowl except the bleu cheese crumbles. Best if made the day before.

Submitted by David Allen

KC MASTERPIECE BARBECUE & GRILL

I-435 & Metcalf
Overland Park, KS 66215
(913) 345-1199

On the Country Club Plaza
47th & Wyandotte
Kansas City, MO
(816) 531-7111

KC Masterpiece® Barbecue and Grill serves outstanding, authentic barbecue and other smoked meats in combination with original, premium side-dishes and desserts. An emphasis on authentic barbecue cooking distinguishes KC Masterpiece® Restaurants from their competition. At the restaurants all meat is grilled or smoked using 100% hickory wood. While barbecue is the featured offering, the restaurants also offer homemade soups, salads, grilled chicken, fish and premium steaks. Many of these original items like Onion Straws, Doc's Dip, KCM Baked Beans and the Chocolate Peanut Butter Ice Cream Pie have received the praise of customers and press alike for their mouth-watering flavors for over 18 years.

Basic Dry Rub

Feel free to experiment! Omit the salt, cut ingredients in half, or add seasoned garlic or onion salts. Keep trying until you get a combination that works for you.

1/2 Cup Brown Sugar
1/2 Cup Paprika
1/2 Cup Celery Salt

1/2 Cup Coarsley Ground Black Pepper
1/4 Cup Chili Powder
2 Tbsp. Garlic Powder

Directions

Combine all ingredients and rub into meat before barbecuing. Makes about 2 cups.

Barbecued Baked Beans

2 (16 oz.) Cans Pork-and-Beans, Drained
3/4 Cup KC Masterpiece BBQ Sauce (original
1 Tart Apple, Peeled, Seeded, and Chopped
   (Jonathan or Granny Smith)
3 Strips Uncooked Bacon, Cut in Half
   (or substitute 2 Tbsp. Butter)

1/2 Cup Brown Sugar
1 Tsp. Ground Cumin
1/2 Tsp. Ground Red Pepper
1 oz. Golden Raisins
1 Medium Onion, Chopped

Directions

Preheat oven to 350 degrees. Combine all ingredients except bacon in a 2-quart baking dish. Top with bacon (or dots of butter) and bake uncovered for 1 hour. Serves 6-8.

Submitted by Rich Davis

RC'S RESTAURANT & LOUNGE

330 E. 135th Street
Kansas City, MO (Martin City)
(816) 942-4999
Lunch: Mon-Sat 11 a.m. - 3 p.m.
Dinner: Sun-Thur 11 a.m. - 9:30 p.m.
Fri & Sat 11 a.m. - 10 p.m.

R.C.'s Restaurant & Lounge, Inc., was started in 1973 by Raymond Charles VanNoy, Jr. (R.C. for short). A 25-year veteran of National Cash Register, he also worked part time for his cousin nights and weekends at Jess & Jim's Steak House in Martin City.

The original building where the restaurant was located was formerly a machine shop. R.C. turned it into a restaurant which seated 100 in the dining room and 35 in the lounge.

R.C.'s first achieved renown for its lounge and jukebox. R.C. then hired a well-known pan fried chicken specialist, red headed Betty Lucas. Betty taught R.C.'s three sons, Chuck, David and Mike, all the secrets of serving a homemade family-style friend chicken dinner.

The restaurant became a family operation with R.C. managing, his wife doing bookwork, his daughter waiting tables and his three sons cooking. The friend chicken meals were so good that on Friday and Saturday, people waiting in line for a table would sit with strangers so they could all eat faster.

R.C. became the owner of Jess & Jim's Steak House, leaving his restaurant to be run by his sons. The boys increased business so much that they moved to a bigger and better building across the street from the original R.C.'s which opened on New Year's Eve 1982.

R.C.'s now has two stories, seating 185 downstairs, 85 in the lounge and 250 upstairs in R.C. Back Door Bar.

R.C. House Vinegar & Oil Salad Dressing

1 Family size can of tomato soup	1 Family size can of salad oil
1-2/3 cans vinegar	4 oz. sugar
2 oz. salt	1/2 oz. garlic, minced
1 oz. onion-minced	1-1/2 dashes Worcestershire sauce

Directions

Mix together and toss on salad or you can use as a steak marinate.

Submitted by the VanNoy Family

ROMANELLI GRILL & BAR

**7122 Wornall Road
Kansas City, MO
(816) 333-1321**

A former A&P grocery store, the Romanelli Grill & Bar has been a fixture in Brookside, MO since 1935. The present owner, Joe MacCabe Jr., makes it his goal to keep Romanelli's a place where neighborhood folks can meet and eat good food. Once you enter this local favorite you discover the secret to their time-honored traditions and loyal patronage: Home-style cooking and service with a smile and then some. Eat here a couple of times, and they'll know your usual order

Red Mushroom Sauce

2 oz. Fresh Garlic (chopped)	2 oz. Fresh Shallots (chopped)
1/3 Cup Dry White Vermouth	1/2 Cup Sugar
1 Can (diced) Tomatoes (14.5 oz.)	1 Can (crushed) Tomatoes (15 oz.)
1 Can Tomato Paste (12 oz.)	24 oz. Water
1 Tsp. Fennel Powder	2 Tbsp. Crushed Oregano
3 Tbsp. Crushed Sweet Basil	1 Tbsp. Salt
3/4 Tbsp. Fresh Cracked Black Pepper	8 oz. Fresh Mushrooms (sliced)

Directions

Heat garlic and shallots in olive oil until soft. Add vermouth and simmer, about 3 minutes. Add all the rest of the ingredients and cook on very low heat for about 2 hours, stirring constantly. Sauce is now ready to serve.

Submitted by Joe MacCabe Jr.

ROSATI'S PIZZA

516 W. 103rd Street
Kansas City, MO 64114
(816) 941-6363
Fax (816) 941-6699

6485 Quivira Road
Shawnee, KS 66216
(913) 962-6262
Fax (913) 962-4940

Started in 1964, Rosati's has always strived to provide the best of what Chicago is famous for: Pizza, Italian Beef and Hot Dogs. To carry on this legacy we use only the freshest ingredients, prepared daily, to produce our fare. Delivery and Pick-up only. Our menu has something for everyone.

The Cheef Sandwich/Au Jus

1 Large Green Pepper (Chopped)
4 oz. Minced Garlic
2 oz. Olive Oil
1 Tbsp. Salt
2 Tbsp. Oregano
2 Crusty French Bread
2 oz. Hot Giardineva

1 Medium Onion (Chopped)
4 oz. Hot Giardineva Pepper
2 oz. Red Pepper Flake
1 Tbsp. Pepper
1 lb. Sliced (Thin) Beef Roast (rare)
1 Gallon Beef Stock
4 oz. Grated Mozzarella Cheese

Directions

In a large stock pot heat oil. Add green pepper, onion, garlic and 4 oz. Giardineva pepper. Over medium heat sweat ingredients for 5 minutes (stir occasionally). Add spices and continue to sweat 5 minutes. Add beef stock and reduce to medium-low heat. Simmer uncovered for 1 hour (minimum). DO NOT BOIL. Strain through a fine mesh strainer into a sauce pan.

Add thin sliced beef and allow to stand for 30-45 seconds, remove. Place beef into sliced French loaf, top with 2 oz. Giardineva pepper and Mozzarella cheese. Place in oven on broil until cheese melts. Remove sandwiches and dip the ends into the au jus. Serve and enjoy!

Submitted by Mark Wright

SMOKIN' JOE'S BAR-B-Q & CATERING

101 Southwest Blvd.
Kansas City, MO 64108
(816) 421-2282 Fax (816) 421-3532
On the SW Corner of 19th & Baltimore

Visit our other location at City Center Square Food Court

> "In 1988 I wanted to get some good ribs, but I didn't think anybody had good ribs. So I bought a Bar-B-Q and did it myself and am still going strong."
> *Ralph Sander, Smokin' Joe's Bar-B-Q*

Joe's Baked Beans

3 Cups Light Molasses
1/2 #10 Can Ketchup
.30 (scale) Chile Powder
4 #10 Cans Pork & Beans

3/4 Gallon Joe's BBQ Sauce
1 qt. Dark Brown Sugar
.15 (scale) Instant Onions
6 Lbs. Chopped Beef

Directions

Mix well the first 6 ingredients, and beans and beef and fold into sauce. Place in pit under beef brisket only and smoke until temperature reaches 145 degrees.

Joe's Cole Slaw

Yields approx. 35 lbs.
1-1/2 Gallons of Mayonnaise
1 qt. Granulated Sugar
.04 (scale) Ground Black Pepper
.35 (scale) Distilled White Vinegar
1/2 the amount of carrots that come with the cabbage.

Sour Cream
Garlic Powder
.05 (scale) Whole Celery Seed
4 Bags Shredded White Cabbage

Directions

Mix well the first 7 ingredients, add cabbage and carrots and fold into dressing.

Submitted by Ralph Sander

STEPHENSON'S APPLE FARM RESTAURANT

16401 E. HIGHWAY 40
KANSAS CITY, MO. 64133
(816) 373-5400 • (816) 373-2228

A Little About the Apple Farm Restaurant. Like most early Missouri settlers, our grandparents smoked meats, made apple butter, canned their own fruits and vegetables. And so, on April 16, 1946, when we opened the original stone building, it seemed natural to call it The Apple Farm. We had 10 booths then and served 38 people the first day. Then, as now , we served old-fashioned hickory smoked meats, homemade apple butter, preserves and relishes – all prepared in our kitchens in the unique manner which our grandparents had taught us. We join the young men and women who are serving you in a warm welcome.

Sunday Family Chicken Dinner and Fried Catfish Dinner served 11:00AM to 9:00PM. Off Premises Catering We will Cater to your office, church, park, backyard, etc. Beautiful Private Banquet Rooms Our Manager will be glad to show you around.

Side dish here at Stephenson's, very popular!

Scalloped Zucchini Casserole

Makes 6-8 Servings
Heat to Scalding:

1C Hot Milk	1 T Butter
1 Chicken Bouillon Cube	

Mix the Following:

2 Eggs Beaten	2 # diced fresh Zucchini

1 T each; Chopped Pimento, Chopped Onion, Chopped Green Pepper

1/4 C Bread Crumbs	1/4 T Salt

Dash of Pepper

Directions

Blend with Milk Mixture and bake in 1-1/2 Qt Baking Dish at 325 degrees for about 1 hour.

Submitted by Stephenson's Kitchens

THE MELTING POT

450 Ward Parkway
Kansas City, MO 64112
(816) 931-6358
Fax (816) 531-3251

The Melting Pot opened on The Country Club Plaza in December 2001. Many have enjoyed the ambience of dark wood and candles with cozy booths and tables for large parties. Since opening, we have designed private dining rooms for couples to enjoy, including champagne, limosine service and carriage rides. Sunday through Friday from 4p to 7p in our lounge, you can partake in our Happy Hour with half price cheese and chocolate fondue and discounted drink prices. We are open seven days a week for dinner, closing at 10:30p Sun-Thurs and 11:30p Fri-Sat.

Wisconsin Trio Cheese Fondue

3 oz. Domestic white wine   1 oz. Sherry (3 to 4 oz. total base)
1 demitasse spoon Shallots
50 Fantina Cheese, 50 Butterkase (to consistency approx. 10 oz.)
7 turns Ground pepper   1 oz. Buttermilk Bleu Cheese
Scallions garnish with 3 demitasse spoons

Directions

Once the fondue pot has come to a full steam, add base of white wine and sherry. Then add 1 demitasse spoon of shallots. Stir. Then start adding cheese, the blend of Fontina and Butterkase. Add cheese a little at a time to allow to melt.

While adding the cheese, fold the cheese. After cheese is all added, then add the 7 turns of ground pepper. Fold the pepper into the cheese. Then add 1 oz. Buttermilk Bleu Cheese and fold into cheese. Garnish with 3 demitasse spoons of scallions. We serve this cheese with Granny Smith apples, French, Rye, Pumpernickel Bread and fresh vegetables.

Submitted by Donn Davis

THE SCHOOL HOUSE BAR & GRILL

7938 Santa Fe
Overland Park, KS 66204
(913) 385-9908
TheSchoolHouseBar.com

Located in the heart of old downtown Overland Park, the School House continues the rich tradition of this great area and building which it calls home.

This sports bar & grill offers a fun concept and unique setting in which to enjoy your favorite spirits and food from the School House's varied menu. With choices ranging from tantalizing buffalo wings, a variety of wraps and salads, delicious sandwiches, KC Strip steaks and meatloaf to their signature School House Burger, the School House offers something for almost everyone!

A large venue with over 25 TV's including 3 giant screens & varying entertainment every night makes it a must see spot for Sports, parties, or just unwinding after a long day of work.

Seth's Sweet Sloppy Joes

2 lbs ground beef browned and lightly salted
2 cans Campbell's chicken gumbo soup
3/4 to 1 cup of brown sugar depending on desired sweetness
1/8 cup mustard
2/3 to 3/4 cup ketchup
1/3 cup Quaker oats (not instant

Directions

Combine ground beef, gumbo, mustard & ketchup over a medium heat. Bring to a slow boil then add brown sugar and oatmeal and reduce heat to low. Simmer for 10 minutes, stirring often. Remove from heat and let cool for 10 minutes.

Good toppings include Cheddar cheese and pickles.

Submitted by School House Bar & Grill

BAR & GRILL

22730 Midland Drive
Shawnee, KS
S.E. Corner of 7 Hwy. & Shawnee Mission Pkwy.
(913) 422-8356
www.zigandmacs.com

This state-of-the-art high energy sports bar offers an eclectic dining experience featuring New American Cuisine with traditional pub fare. The variety of the menu will become a palate pleaser, offering a great dining experience to our guests. Our patrons can savor Thai Lettuce Wraps, Parmesan Encrusted Talapia, Mac's Cobb Salad, Shrimp scampi Au gratin, Southwest Cavitappi, Vermont Maple Pork Loin, Chicken Piccata, and the Crescent City Pizza to name a few. There is something to appeal to even the most discriminating diner. The 24 televisions will always allow the sports enthusiast to be "In the Zone." Our 35+ seat Banquet Rooms and Patio can accommodate a variety of theme events.

Corn Crab Cake Mix

Servings: 16
Preparation time: 15 minutes

2 1/2 pounds crab meat
1 cup red onion, minced
1 ounce chives, minced
3 cups bread crumbs
1 tablespoon sugar
1 tablespoon black pepper
1/2 cup dijon mustard

2 cups corn kernels, roasted
1 each red bell pepper, minced
3 cups mayonnaise
1/8 cup sherry
1 tablespoon lemon juice
5 each eggs, lightly beaten
1/8 cup old Bay Seafood seasoning

Directions

In a large mixing bowl add the crab meat chopping it up and squeezing all the water out, but still leaving some large chunks. Puree corn with mayo. Add all the remaining ingredients and fold together until incorporated. Label, date, and refrigerate. Yield: 1 gallon.

Place two tablespoons of olive oil in skillet and sauté in batches until golden brown. Add olive oil as needed.

Submitted by J.R. Sutton

RESTAURANT

DESSERTS

Family Made Just For You.

Kansas City's finest restaurants know quality. Which is why they feature the premium line of Belfonte dairy products and ice cream. Here's to good eating, from our family to yours!

Family Made Just For You.

1625 Cleveland, Kansas City, Missouri 64127
www.belfontedairy.com

ANDRÉ'S CONFISERIE SUISSE

Dark Bittersweet Truffles

Ganache
1 Cup Heavy Cream
1.5 oz. Unsalted Butter (softened)
8 oz. Cocoa Powder
40-50 truffles Yields approximately

1 lb. Dark Chocolate (chopped)
8 oz. Dark Chocolate for finishing
Powder Sugar for Rolling

Directions

Bring cream to a low boil then remove from heat. Stir in the chocolate which has been chopped into small pieces. When the chocolate has melted add the softened butter and stir until smooth. Pour into a clean, dry bowl and cover with stretch film or wax paper.

Allow the mixture to cool and solidify. Place semi solid mixture into a piping bag with a medium round piping tube. Pipe half rounds the size of a quarter onto wax paper then refrigerate until cool and firm. When firm remove from refrigerator and roll into balls using powder sugar or cocoa powder to coat your hands so that the ganache does not stick. Roll quickly because if you have warm hands the filling will soften and become sticky! Once the ball has been formed place back onto the wax paper.

When all the half rounds have been transformed into balls place them into the refrigerator to cool. Melt the 8 oz. of finishing chocolate in a double boiler or microwave. When melted but not too warm (90 degrees F), coat the cool ganache balls with a very thin coating of chocolate. Apply a small amount of chocolate to each hand and then roll one ball at a time between your hands until evenly coated. Place the coated ball into a flat pan with a 1/4 inch coating of cocoa powder. Using a spatula roll the ball in the cocoa until totally coated. Leave on the pan in the cocoa until the chocolate has become firm. Then place onto a sift and gently sift off the excess cocoa powder.

These delicate chocolate Truffles should be eaten within one week or they may be placed into an air tight container and refrigerated or frozen for later consumption. When removing from the refrigerator or freezer, allow to return to room temperature before opening the air tight seal to avoid condensation on the Truffles.

Yields approximately 40-50 truffles.

Submitted by Marcel & Connie Bollier

CASCONE'S ITALIAN RESTAURANT

3733 North Oak Trafficway
Kansas City, MO
(816) 454-7977

TUTTO LA FAMIGLIA

The Cascone Family has been in the restaurant business for over 60 years. Beginning with a small diner on Locust Trafficway near downtown Kansas City, MO. Now there are three restaurants in the area run by the Cascone Family and Kansas Citians have made Cascone's their favorite Italian Restaurant, dining on award-winning cuisine which has become the trademark of Cascone's.

Italian Refrigerator Cake

4 Eggs, Separated	1/4 Cup Cold Water
1 Cup Sifted Flour	1/2 Tsp. Lemon Flavoring
1 Tsp. Baking Powder	1 Tsp. Salt
1 Cup Granulated Sugar	1 Tsp. Vanilla

Directions

Set ingredients out for approx. 1 hour before assembling recipe. Beat egg yolks and water together until fluffy. Add sugar, beat for 5 minutes. Fold in flour and salt. Beat egg whites stiff and moist. Fold into yolk and flour mixture until completely blended. Pour into 2 (8 inch) pans, lined with waxed paper and greased. Bake at 350 degrees for 25 to 30 minutes, remove from pans and cool.

Filling: 1 lb Ricotta Cheese and 3/4 cup sugar, beat together until creamy.
Add: 1/3 cup sweet chocolate pieces and 1/3 cup toasted almond slices.

Make one single recipe of your favorite chocolate pudding and 1 of vanilla pudding. Split the cake to make 4 layers. Place 1 layer on cake plate, cut side up. Spread with chocolate pudding. For second layer, spread Ricotta filling. Finally for the last layer spread vanilla pudding. Frost final cake with sweetened whipped cream.

Submitted by Jimmy Cascone

CHICKEN-N-BLUES

235 S.E. Main St.
Lee's Summit, MO
(816) 246-0600

Chicken-N-Blues is located in the historic shopping district in Downtown Lee's Summit. We offer pan fried chicken just like a country grandmother would make. Excellent home style country fried steaks, whole catfish and catfish fillets, tender gizzards and livers. Chicken-N-Blues is open Sunday 8 a.m. to 11 a.m. for breakfast and 11 a.m. to 2 p.m. for dinner. Wednesday and Thursday 11 a.m. to 8 p.m. and Friday and Saturday 11 a.m. to 9 p.m. We are closed Monday and Tuesday. Chicken-N-Blues is a non-smoking restaurant.

Grandma's Bread Pudding

3 Cups Whipping Cream
8 Eggs Slightly Beaten
4 Tbs. Melted Butter
1/2 Cup Butter Melted
1-1/2 lb. Day Old Bread (Italian bread or hotdog buns)

3 Cups Milk
4 Cups Sugar (white or brown)
2 Tbs. Cinnamon
1 Tbs. Vanilla Extract

Directions

Cut bread into medium cubes. Soak in milk for 10 minutes. Combine eggs, sugar, butter, vanilla and cinnamon. Add to bread crumbs. Spray pan with vegetable oil, add mixture.

Pour melted butter over top. Cover with foil and bake 45 minutes at 350 degrees.

Submitted by Dan Dannaldson

EBT RESTAURANT

EBT

1310 Carondelet Drive
(I-435 & State Line)
Kansas City, MO
(816) 942-8870 • www.EBTrestaurant.com

EBT is a Kansas City tradition that was originally run by Myron Green Cafeteria's and is now run by Treat America Food Services, which has been nominated in One Of The Top Ten Small Businesses of Kansas City for 2005. EBT's is a full service restaurant that offers lunch and dinner along with a private room that holds up to 50 people for special occasions or business meetings for reservations please call 816-942-8870.

Banana's Foster

2 T. Butter
1.5 oz. banana Liqueur
1.5 oz. Bacardi 151
2 Scoop Vanilla Ice Cream

6 T. Brown Sugar
1 Banana, Quartered
Dash Cinnamon

Directions

Melt butter in a pan over medium heat, add brown sugar and banana liqueur, and cook slowly for several minutes until sugar dissolves, making a caramel sauce.

Add quartered banana's and pour in 151 (close to the edge) and flame.

Lightly sprinkle cinnamon over flame for sparkle effect.

Sauté for 1 minute and spoon over ice cream. Yield: 2 portions

Submitted by EBT

CROWN CENTER RESTAURANTS BY HYATT
Golden Harvest Bakery
2450 Grand Street
Kansas City, MO 64108
(816) 435-4128, Fax (816) 435-4153

Do you have a sweet tooth? If so, you'll LOVE Golden Harvest Bakery. It is conveniently located on the first floor of the Crown Center shops and serves as a retail bakery specializing in breads, breakfast pastries, sandwiches, salads, gourmet coffee, cakes, cookies and more.

Golden Harvest Bakery Sugar Cookies

1 lb. Butter
1-1/2 lbs. Sugar
4 Eggs

4 lb. and 1/4 cup All Purpose Flour
3/4 oz. Baking Powder
3/4 oz. Cream of tartar

Directions

With a mixer, cream together sugar and butter. Add eggs until well combined. Sift all of the dry ingredients together. Add dry ingredients to butter, sugar, and egg mixture until the dough comes together. Scoop into 3 ounce balls and bake at 325 degrees until edges start to brown. Do not overcook.

Submitted by Dominic Vaccaro, Executive Sous Chef, CCRH

HEREFORD HOUSE

20th & Main, Kansas City, MO • (816) 842-1080
5001 Town Center Drive, Leawood, KS • (913) 327-0800
4931 W. 6th Street, Lawrence, KS • (785) 842-2333
19721 E. Jackson Dr., Independence, MO • (816) 795-9200
Zona Rosa – 8661 Stoddard, North Kansas City, MO 64153 • (816) 584-9000

Very few American steakhouses come close to the consistent excellence and quality standards that The Hereford House has mastered for nearly 48 years. Even fewer have earned the national reputation that makes this independent restaurant a favorite of legendary sports figures, Hollywood celebrities and even a few U.S. Presidents.

What's our secret? Sterling Silver Premium Beef. It comes from premium cattle bred and raised in the high plains of North America. We like to say that Hereford House beef makes life taste better.

With five locations around the metro area, you'll never find yourself too far away from this Kansas City tradition. Go ahead. Consider tonight's dinner plans made. Fire up your car and head over to one of our area restaurants. We'll fire up our grill for the best steak dinner you've ever enjoyed. See you at the Hereford House!

Strawberry Shortcake

1 5-lb. Bag Bisquick Mix,	3-1/2 Cups Whole Milk
1-1/4 lb. Melted Butter	1-1/4 Cup Sugar
2 Qts. Strawberries, Sliced	2 Cups Sugar

Directions

Melt the butter and add to the milk. Blend the bisquit mix and the sugar together with a wire whip to blend well. Add the milk and butter mix to the batter mix and stir well to form a soft dough. Using a #10 scoop, scoop biscuits onto an ungreased sheet tray and bake in the convection oven until browned and cooked.

Remove the stems and the tops from the fresh strawberries. Slice the strawberries into 1/4" strips, and place in a plastic storage container. Cover the strawberries with the sugar, and gently mix to coat.

Let the strawberries rest, under refrigeration for at least 4 hours. This will allow for the strawberries to form their own syrup.

Place the prepared shortcake biscuit on a baking dish and brush with 1 tablespoon of melted butter. Sprinkle the biscuit with 1 tsp. granulated sugar and place in a 350-degree oven for 1-2 minutes to heat the biscuit.

Remove from the oven and place in the center of the service platter. Place 1 scoop of ice cream next to the biscuit at 3:00. Cover the biscuit and the ice cream with 3/4 cup of sliced sugared strawberries and their syrup.

Pipe out the whipped cream into 3 1-oz. rosettes at 6:00, 9:00 and 12:00 on the platter. Garnish with a sprig of mint and serve.

Submitted by Hereford House

IVY'S RESTAURANT

240 N. E. Barry Road
Kansas City, MO 64155
(816) 436-3320
Fax (816) 436-3329

Ivy's was started in 1977 by Sam and Carol Cross. We offer Poultry, Steaks, Prime Rib, Seafood and Pasta. The Pasta Kitchen is a favorite entree to have when visiting Ivy's. The chef prepares the dish with one of your favorite sauces, pasta and many vegetables and meat choices. You can make it spicy, with lots of garlic or as plain as you want.

We also offer live jazz on Friday and Saturday from 6:30 p.m. to 10 p.m. This is a separate dining area in the restaurant. We also offer private dining rooms for 8 to 80. Ivy's was voted the most romantic restaurant in the Northland and received many awards for food and wine.

Cream Cheese Ice Cream

4 Cups Cream
24 Egg Yolks
3 Cups Sour Cream
4 Tsp. Vanilla

2-1/2 Cups Sugar
24 oz. Cream Cheese
    (cubed and at room temperature)
Pinch of Salt

Directions

Temper cream with 2 cups sugar, combine 1/2 cup sugar and the yolks. When the sugar is dissolved in the cream combine the cream to the yolks and put back on the double boiler and constantly stir on medium heat until it coats the back of a spoon (about 8 minutes). Take off heat and add the cream cheese, sour cream, salt, and vanilla. Once the cream cheese is melted strain and cool.

Submitted by Ivy's Restaurant

6863 W. 91st St.
Overland Park, KS 66212
(913) 381-6837
Fax (913) 381-7587

TUTTO LA FAMIGLIA

The Cascone Family has been in the restaurant business for over 60 years. Beginning with a small diner on Locust Trafficway near downtown Kansas City, MO. Now there are three restaurants in the area run by the Cascone Family and Kansas Citians have made Cascone's their favorite Italian Restaurant, dining on award-winning cuisine which has become the trademark of Cascone's.

Chocolate Cannoli Shells

1 Lb. Flour
1 Tbsp. Cornstarch
1 Whole Egg
3/4 Cup Milk
1 Lbs. Crisco (for frying)

1 Tbsp. Cocoa
1/2 Cup Crisco
1/2 Cup Sugar
1 Quart Crisco Oil (for frying)

Directions

Mix first 4 ingredients in stainless steel bowl. Melt sugar in lukewarm milk. With your hands, mix all dry ingredients together then add milk, sugar and beaten egg. Work dough until it's smooth.

Roll out into thin small circles, do not add additional flour when rolling. Wrap each circle around an aluminum cannoli tube. (Available at most gourmet food stores) Overlap the dough about 1 inch and attach ends with milk.

Preheat Crisco oil and Crisco to about 325 degrees in an electric fryer. Cook each cannoli tube for about 1/2 to 1 minute or until nice and brown. Cool and remove from tube. Use desired Ricotta Filling.

FILLING RECIPE:

2 Lbs. Ricotta Cheese (well drained)
1 Cup Cream Beaten Stiff
1 Tsp. Vanilla

1 Cup Sugar
1.2 Cup Hershey's Bar (cut up fine)

Beat Ricotta cheese with whip, adding sugar gradually until smooth. (Do not over beat) Add vanilla and fold into whipped cream. Add chopped Hershey Bar. Refrigerate overnight. Fill shells when ready to serve.

Maraschino cherries, cut up and blotted dry, and nuts can be added to this filling is desired.

Submitted by Jimmy Cascone

JUMPIN CATFISH RESTAURANT

1861 S. Ridgeview
Olathe, KS
(913) 829-FISH (3474)

4342 NE Antioch Rd.
Kansas City, MO
(816) 452-FISH (3474)

834 SW Blue Parkway
Lee's Summit, MO
(816) 554-FISH (3474)

Our restaurant started almost 19 years ago by David Hampton (owner) to satisfy a craving for catfish and southern cooking in the Kansas City area. Dinners are served family style with all-you-can-eat specials every night. Through the years we have expanded our menu to over 75 items. We specialize in catfish, chicken, seafood and wild game.

Lemon Ice Box Pie

1-1/2 Cans Eagle Brand Sweetened Condensed Milk
4 Eggs (separate the whites)
1/2 Cup Lemon Juice
1/4 Tsp. Cream of Tartar for Meringue

1-9" Graham Crust
1/2 Cup Sugar

Directions

Beat the 4 yolks, add condensed milk and lemon juice. Mix well and pour into graham crust. Bake in oven at 350 degrees until brown (approx. 20-30 minutes).

For meringue beat egg whites slightly then add sugar gradually with 1/4 tsp. cream of tartar. (Also can be topped with whipped cream)

Submitted by Sean Johnston

MARGARITA'S AUTHENTIC MEXICAN FOOD

Margarita's
Authentic Mexican Food

7013 N. Oak
Gladstone, MO
(816) 468-0337

2829 Southwest Blvd.
Kansas City, MO
(816) 931-4849

12200 Johnson Dr.
Shawnee, KS
(913) 631-5553

13401 Holmes
Kansas City, MO
(816) 941-9411

There are many aspects to Margarita's success. One is their philosophy that "the customer is number one." There is something to please everyone on their extensive menu. Another is old family recipes that help Chef John Abarca to dish up authentic Mexican food that melts in your mouth and keeps customers loyal and coming back. They pride themselves on using the best products and ingredients they can buy. Let's not forget where Margarita's got its name. It is named for the popular Mexican drink that contains tequila, triple sec and other ingredients. At the restaurant Margarita's are made in large batches then dispensed through a tap like draught beef. When you go to Margarita's you know you will get good service, drinks, and most importantly good food, in short it feels like coming home.

Margarita's Arroz con Leche

2 Cups Heavy Cream
1 Cup White Rice
1/8 tsp. Salt
1 Cup Sugar
1 Tbsp. Whipped Cream

1 Cups Milk
2 Sticks Cinnamon
2 Cups Half and Half
1 Tbsp. Orange Zest
1 Tbsp. Ground Cinnamon

Directions

Combine heavy cream, milk, cinnamon sticks, salt, orange zest and rice and bring it up to a boil, then down to a simmer about 30 minutes or until the rice is cooked. In a separate pan heat the half and half and add to the rice mixture and stir at a simmer. Take off the heat and add sugar and mix well. Strain and remove cinnamon sticks. Take excess milk and whip for whipped cream. Garnish with whipped cream and cinnamon.

Submitted by David and Ron

PIERPONT'S

Fresh Seafood • Prime Steaks

Located in Union Station
(816) 221-5111
www.pierponts.com

Named for the railroad baron, J.P. (John Pierpont) Morgan, Pierpont's 1914 decor combined with 21st century innovation offers you old world elegance with contemporary flair.

This is your very special invitation to experience Pierpont's at Union Station. It's been dubbed "the culinary jewel" of Kansas City's historically renovated Union Station, and has earned the reputation of serving Kansas City's finest steak and seafood selections.

As a sister restaurant to the legendary Hereford House, Pierpont's maintains the family tradition of serving prime steak, perfectly aged and prepared. With fresh seafood arriving daily, an award winning wine list, and the unique creations of some of the areas finest chefs, Pierpont's has been named "Best Place to Entertain Guests" and "Best Place to take a Group" from the local press.

In addition to dining room seating, your smaller party will enjoy the private Wine Cellar rooms, while larger banquets overlook the grand dining room below. Reservations are always honored, but not required. www.herefordhouse.com

Chocolate Torte

Yield: 1 - 10" Torte

1 lb. Unsalted Butter	2.5 Cups Semi-Sweet Chocolate
1 Cup Strong Coffee (or Espresso)	1 Cup Sugar
7 Eggs	

Directions

In a heavy bottomed saucepan, over low heat, melt butter. Add coffee and chocolate and whisk until melted and smooth. Cool mixture slightly.

In a large bowl combine eggs and sugar. Slowly add chocolate mixture, whisking until combined. Strain through a fine sieve.

Line the inside of a 10" springform pan with parchment paper. Spray with nonstick cooking spray. Line outside of pan with foil.

Bake at 350 degrees for 40-45 minutes. Will look like a cheesecake, set on the outsides but still a little wobbly in the center.

Cool. Refrigerate. Enjoy.

Submitted by Pierpont's

Sutera's

22716 Midland Drive
Shawnee, KS 66226
(913) 667-3000 • Fax (913) 667-3040

1617 Genessee
Kansas City, MO
(816) 471-8909

Sutera's opened its first restaurant in the west bottoms in 1976, in time for the Republican Convention. Since then Sutera's has opened locations in Bonner Springs, Shawnee and is a opening a new restaurant soon in Westwood.
Best Pizza in town!

Biscotti's (Italian Cookies)

6 Cups Flour
2-1/2 Tbsp. Baking Powder
2-1/4 Cup Sugar
2-1/2 Cup Crisco or Lard

1/2 Dozen Eggs
1/4 Cup Vanilla
Milk as Needed
Sesame Seeds

Directions

Mix dry ingredients. Add lard and eggs. Beat with your hand. Add vanilla. Take a piece of dough and roll into sesame seeds 4" long and as wide as your finger. bake at 375 Degrees for 15 minutes.

Submitted by Aunt Busilacci from Milwaukee, 90 years old

The Chocolate Store

11500 W. 90th Street
Overland Park, KS 66214
(913) 541-2021
Fax (913) 541-2031

The Chocolate Store offers French, Beligan and Swiss Chocolate. White, dark and milk chocolate are available in chips, chunks and blocks for cooking and confections. You can purchase them by the pound. The Chocolate Store is a division of Mid America Gourmet, Kansas City's wholesale supplier of European pastry ingredients. We are conveniently located next to our warehouse at 90th & Bond, between Quivira and Nieman Road. We're open Monday through Friday from 8 a.m. to 5 p.m.

Hawaiian Vintage Chocolate Brownies

5 oz. Hawaiian Vintage Bittersweet Chocolate
1-1/4 Cups Sifted All-Purpose Flour
1/2 Tsp. Salt
2 Extra Large Eggs
6 Tbsp. Unsalted Butter
1/2 Tsp. Baking Powder
3/4 Cup + 2 Tbsp. Very Fine Sugar
1 Cup Walnuts, Coarsley Chopped

Directions

TO PREPARE THE PAN: Grease and line an 8-inch square baking pan with wax or parchment paper. Grease paper and flour. Preheat oven to 350 degrees.

TO PREPARE THE BATTER: Melt the chocolate and butter in a microwave oven stirring every 15 seconds, remove from the heat before fully melted and continue to stir. Allow the chocolate to cool just until no hotter than lukewarm.

In a small bowl, whisk together the flour, baking powder and salt. Gradually add the sugar, eggs, and then flour mixture to the chocolate. Mix well. Stir in nuts.

Pour batter into the prepared pan and bake 30 to 35 minutes or until a toothpick inserted in the center comes out almost clean. The brownies should still be slightly moist in the center.

Unmold the brownies on a flat surface. When cool, cut the brownies into 2 inch squares. To preserve moisture, wrap each brownie in plastic wrap.

Submitted by Jen Geis

THE PIZZA MAN

The Pizza Man

10212 Pflumm Road
Lenexa, Kansas 66215
(913) 492-2116

Hours:
Mon.-Thurs. 11 a.m. - 9 p.m.
Friday 11 a.m. - 10 p.m.
Saturday 12 p.m. to 10 p.m.
Sunday 2 p.m. - 8 p.m.

The Pizza Man – Lenexa's best kept secret. Located 1/2 block north of 103rd St. on Pflumm, serving a thin crust Chicago style pizza since 1988.

We also have sandwiches: Chicago hotdogs, Italian beef, Italian sausage, meatball, Polish sausage, Reuben, roast beef, 1/2 lb. burgers and a few more.

Stop by and give us a try.

Kansas Dirt

8-10 oz. whole milk
1/2 cup powdered sugar
1/4 stick margarine
4-6/5 oz. servings

5 oz. chocolate pudding
4 oz. Philly cream cheese
Crushed Oreo cookie crumbs

Directions

Soften cream cheese and margarine and mix powdered sugar with chocolate pudding. Pour in 5 oz servings and chill for a couple of hours. Then serve.

Kanas Frozen Dirt

Vanilla ice cream, Oreo cookie crumbs, chocolate syrup and milk blended together. Topped with whipped cream, rainbow sprinkles, Oreo cookie.

Directions

Mix together and enjoy.

Submitted by Bob Kranz

THE SAVOY GRILL

SAVOY GRILL

219 W. 9th Street
Kansas City, MO 64105
(816) 842-3890
(816) 221-3131

In 1903 The Savoy Grill dining room opened and today is the oldest restaurant in Kansas City, with stained glass windows, high beamed ceilings, lanterns that were once gaslights and an enormous carved oak bar. Booth No. 4, known as the presidents' booth has been host to Warren Harding, Harry S. Truman, Gerald Ford and Ronald Reagan. The original Grill Room is surrounded by The Savoy Murals, painted by Edward Holslag in 1903 and have been included in the Smithsonian Institution's "Bicentennial Inventory of American Paintings." The Savoy Grill is Kansas City's most popular landmark, serving the best quality steaks and seafood for lunch and dinner.

Crème Brulee

2 qt. heavy cream
2 qt. half and half
2 tsp vanilla

1/2 tsp. nutmeg
15 egg yolks
1 1-lb. super fine sugar

Directions

Whip eggs and 1/2 lb. sugar till twice the size. Heat milk, vanilla, nutmeg and 1/2 lb. sugar–do not boil. Mix together slowly. Put in baking cups. Put cups in water bath at 350 degrees for 1 hour and 15 minutes. When firm remove from oven and cool for 2 hours. Makes 20 cups.

Submitted by Don Lee

WAID'S FAMILY RESTAURANTS

6920 Mission Rd.
Prairie Village, KS
(913) 362-2882

1130 W. 103rd
Kansas City, MO
(816) 942-1354

Our tradition of quality, service and value began in 1953. Serving breakfast, lunch and dinner for over 50 years, we start with the highest quality ingredients preparing our own original recipes right on the premises. Great home style foods served in a friendly, comfortable atmosphere is what makes Waid's value greater than ever.

Famous Strawberry Pie

1 lb. Powdered Sugar   2-1/2 oz. Corn Starch,
Mix corn starch and sugar and set aside.
Will be enough for 3 pies.

1 Prebaked Pie Shell
32 oz. Strawberries, fresh and stemmed, (Makes 1 Pie)
1 cup Powdered Sugar Mix (from above)
Whipped Cream as needed

Directions

Place strawberries and sugar mixture in round mixing bowl. Blend carefully with rubber spatula keeping the strawberries in tact. Pour strawberries in prebaked pie shell and top with whipped cream. Makes one pie.

Submitted by Paul D. Russell

RESTAURANT
BEVERAGES

8550 W. 151st St.
Overland Park, KS 66223
(913) 897-0033
Fax (913) 897-0940

www.cccitybroiler.com

C.C.'s City Broiler exclusively serves some of the best USDA Prime Graded Midwestern corn-fed beef. Our filet mignons are barrel cut on the premises ensuring the finest quality. Our Veal Chops and Pork Chops are always Center Cut and our Rack of Lamb is the best New Zealand has to offer.

Our chefs season to perfection and capture Ultimate flavor and tenderness at 1800 degrees on our special Oak Fired Grill and then top each steak with our famous "Casino Butter." We are sure you will agree that our Steaks and Chops are distinctly Award-Winning.

Fresh Atlantic Salmon, delicate and flavorful Giant Shrimp and Cold Water Lobster highlight a Succulent Seafood Selection. Save room for our Made From Scratch Desserts.

Your table is waiting!

Razzberry Martini

Pour the following into a shaker with ice.
3 oz. Chambord
1 1/2 oz. Absolut Citron
1 1/2 oz. Vanilla Stoli

Shake to the rhythm of you favorite jazz tune.
Strain into a chilled martini glass. Slid a fresh lemon peel around the rim before twisting and dropping into the glass.
Relax and enjoy while your dinner is prepared

Submitted by Luke Entrup

DICK CLARK'S AMERICAN BANDSTAND & GRILL

10975 Metcalf Ave.
Overland Park, KS 66210
(913) 451-1600
Fax (913) 451-4783
www.abgrill.com

Dick Clark's American Bandstand and Grill is located at I-435 and Metcalf. Visitors to our restaurant can enjoy a musical dining experience with selections of our Grill Menu featuring a variety of sandwiches, burgers, and some of Dick Clark's favorite recipes. Meanwhile, guests can groove to their favorite top tunes from the 50s to today, watch music videos and American Bandstand clips and peruse hundreds of pieces of memorabilia including pictures, and gold records.

Guests can dance the night away (21 and up) in our Studio B nightclub.

Dick's Raspberry Long Island

1/4 oz. Smirnoff Raspberry
1/4 oz. Razzmatazz
1/4 oz. Appleton Rum
Splash of Cola

1/4 oz. Cuervo Gold
1/4 oz. Tanquray Gin
Fill with Sour

Serve in Hurricane glass with wedge of lime

Jumpin Jack Flash

1-1/2 oz. Jack Daniels
4 oz. Sour Mix

1/4 oz. Triple Sec

Serve "On the Rocks"

Submitted by Sheila Howell

DINKY & COCO'S CAFÉ

14383 Metcalf Ave.
Overland Park, KS 66223
(913) 897-3800

Dinky & Coco's Cafe', the idea for the business came from a love of both coffee and ice cream from the owner Gale Hammond and the enormous love for her dogs, Dinky and Coco. The store is divided strategically into two sections, one entrance brings you into the Espresso Bar that feautures gourmet brewed coffee from fresh roasted beans and an extensive menu of hot, iced, and frozen espresso beverages. Casual and comfortable seating for about 20 people on this side plus abundant outdoor seating make this a great spot for small business meetings and social get togethers.

Step over to the other side of the store and a whole new world awaits you!! You have entered "Gelato Paradise" where they make homemade Italian Ice Cream in over 100 flavors from the finest ingredients. Dinky & Coco's uses only the most choice quality products imported from Italy. Customers rave about their flavors and incredible quality. They make custom Italian Ice Cream Pies to order and make special order gelato for parties and special events of all kinds. They also make custom gift baskets for all occasions and have gift cards available for purchase.

Fresh Fruit Gelato Smoothie

One pint Dinky & Coco's fresh fruit gelato/sorbet
(any flavor that sounds good to you)
1 cup crushed ice
1 cup milk or lemonade
Fresh fruit garnish or mint leaf

Directions

In order, combine liquid, ice and pint of gelato/sorbet in blender. Blend at high speed for at least 20 seconds to airate well.

Garnish with fresh fruit of choice or a mint leaf. Serve in clear chilled glasses

Submitted by Gale Hammond

ESPRESSO 21 COFFEE SHOP

5401 Johnson Drive
Mission, KS
(913) 403-8571

Connected at the hip from inception, Espresso 21; coffee shop at the Lucky Brewgrille serves only double shot espresso drinks. Well known for its unique drink menu and swanky decor, Espresso 21 parleys the coffeehouse with cigar bar. The menu consists of a variety of flavored coffee drinks and features only Harvey & Son's Premium specialty teas. The coffee shop takes pride in using Kansas City's hometown roaster "Paris Brothers." There is a fresh brewed flavor of the day ranging from French Caramel Cream to Bavarian Chocolate. There is a limited selection of breakfast sandwiches available from 8 a.m. to 11 a.m. Homemade muffins, pastries and bagels line the shelves. The largest humidor in Mission rests in the coffee shop with upscale list of cigars. Open through the week until 8 p.m. and get your day started at 7 a.m. Monday through Friday and 8 a.m. on the weekends. The coffee shop is ideal for an intimate rendezvous or to catch up on current events over hot fresh double Shot Island Mocha Latte and biscotti.

Island Mocha Latte

1 oz. Monin Coconut Syrup
2 oz. Ghirardelli Chocolate
6 oz. Steamed Milk
1 tbsp. Chocolate Shavings

1 oz. Monin Hazelnut Syrup
Double shotEuropean Style Espresso
Whip Cream, fresh

Directions

Fresh grind beans and extract a double shot of espresso. Steam the milk to 140 degrees. In a 12-ounce cup add syrups, chocolate, espresso and only half the steamed milk. Mix thoroughly until chocolate is dissolved. Add the rest of the steamed milk, top with fresh whip cream and chocolate shavings. Enjoy!

Submitted by Greg Fuciu

FOX AND HOUND SMOKEHOUSE & TAVERN

19210-A E 39th Street
Independence, MO 64057
(816) 795.5744
(800) 229.2118 x 6758

10428 Metcalf Ave.
Overland Park, KS
(913) 649-1700
Fax (913) 649-7270

Fox and Hound Smokehouse & Tavern provides a social gathering place offering high quality food, drinks and entertainment in an upscale, casual environment. Our restaurants offer a broad menu of mid-priced appetizers, entrees and desserts served in generous portions. In addition, each location features a full-service bar and offers a wide selection of major domestic, imported and specialty beers.

Raspberry Lemonade

1 oz. Bacardi Limone Rum
Fill with Sweet and Sour Mix

1 oz Chambord Liqueur Royale
Top with Sprite

In Shaker glass mix Bacardi Limone and Chambord with Sweet and Sour and shake vigorously. Pour into pint glass and top with Sprite!

Who Put The Coconut?

1 oz. Malibu Rum
Pineapple juice

1 oz. DeKuyper Pineapple Schnapps
Splash of sprite

In mixing glass combine Malibu, Pineapple schnapps and pineapple juice.
Shake vigorously and put in cocktail glass and top with a splash of
Sprite. Drink & Enjoy!

Submitted by Kristin Caudle

14750 S. Harrison
Olathe, Kansas
(913) 764-0540

1307 S.W. 7 Hwy.
Blue Springs, Missouri
(816) 229-0054

12130 S. 71 Highway
Grandview, Missouri
(816) 965-5454

18700 E. 38th Street
Independence, Missouri
(816) 795-7077

815 S.E. Third Street
Lee's Summit, Missouri
(816) 524-5488

152 Hwy & I-35
Kansas City, Missouri
(816) 792-5489

6332 N.W. Barry Road
Kansas City, Missouri
(816) 587-0864

NEW LOCATION
COMMING SOON!
St. Joseph, Missouri

303 N.E. Englewood Road
Kansas City, Missouri
(816) 455-5609

54th STREET GRILL & BAR

54th Street Grill and Bar is a casual dining restaurant chain founded in 1990 in Kansas City, Missouri by Thomas E. Norsworthy. Tom envisioned an establishment with the kind of quality that exceeded national chain competitors at competitive prices. The result is a nostalgic and cozy atmosphere where the majority of food is made from scratch daily as opposed to the competitor's pre-manufactured products. He also noticed that most concepts concentrated on either the food customer or the bar customer only. While wondering why he couldn't appeal to both groups in the same facility, the 54th Street vision was born.

Through clever architecture and attention to detail he was able to create a facility that accommodates a lively bar crowd with a consistently crowded dining room, translating into a great experience for all.

Black Voodo Rita

1.25 oz. Black Gecko Tequila, 100 proof
1/2 oz. Contreau
1/2 oz. Grand Marnier
8 oz. Sweet-and Sour Mix

Fill a shaker tin with ice. Add above liquors to tin. Add sweet-and-sour mix to tin. Shake to thoroughly mix all ingredients. Garnish serving glass with salt rim and lime wedge.

Big Dawg Bahama Mama

3/4 oz. Malibu rum
3/4 oz. Cremé De Bahama
3 oz. Orange Juice
3/4 oz. Myer's Dark Rum
3 oz. Pineapple Juice
3/4 oz. Grenadine

Fill 18 oz. fish bowl glass with ice. Combine ingredients in above order. Garnish with cherry flag (orange slice, cherry, plastic sword).

Submitted by 54th Street Grill & Bar

JAVA TIME

13344 College Blvd.
Lenexa, Ks 66210
(913) 451-4445

"Simply the Best" is not only our slogan but Java Time is truly the BEST Coffee House at the corner of College & Pflumm in Lenexa, Kansas. Java Time was established on 3 November 2003 has been providing customers with a family friendly atmosphere and exceptional customer service. All of our drinks from a single shot of espresso to smoothies, chai latte's and our very own Javaccino are individually created to provide you the best experience each and every time. Java Times Owners and Professional Barista's take the time to understand your desires in your beverage and ask the questions necessary to meet the need. Java Time serves a select menu of desserts and provides live entertainment from regional artists on the weekends to help you relax after a long week. Our hours are Monday – Thursday 6:30am – 8pm, Friday 6:30am – 9pm, Saturday 7:00am – 9:00pm and Sunday 11:00am – 4:00pm. Hours are subject to change but the Customer Service and Quality will not.

Strawberry Avalon

1/2 cup of brewed coffee
2 oz chocolate syrup
8 oz of milk (whole, 2% or skim)
1 oz of vanilla flavoring (The type used at Java Time to make your favorite drinks)

1/2 cup strawberries (thawed)
1 scoop of vanilla ice cream
1 cup of ice, whipped cream

Directions

In a blender add your coffee, strawberries, chocolate syrup, ice cream, milk, vanilla flavoring and ice. Blend until ingredients are at a smooth texture (Time and power level will vary depending on blender). When smooth pour into a large glass and enjoy. Makes approximately 24 ounces.

Submitted by Master Barista Steven Russell

JEREMIAH JOHNSON'S RESTURANT & TAVERN

5821 NW Barry Rd.
Liberty, MO
(816) 741-3865

Jeremiah Johnson's was opened in June of 2003. Jeremiah Johnson's Restaurant was developed from a prototype of the most popular upscale casual concept in Chicago.

All our steaks and seafood are cooked on an open fire grill using a specially selected grade of oak and hickory timber. We have this timber shipped from a mill that provides restaurant timber for only 4 restaurants in the United States. This unique timber fired cooking approach is what gives Jeremiah's steaks and seafood its one of a kind flavor.

We also offer some of the finest specialties such as our fall-off-the-bone BBQ ribs, specialty chicken and pasta dishes, two-fisted signature sandwiches and unique prepared-to-order salads. All our unique recipes were developed in conjunction with one of the most awarded chefs in the country, Felix Stuermer.

Ultimate Orange Margarita

2 oz. Herradura Tequila
1/4 oz. Contreau
3 oz. Fresh Squeezed Orange Juice

3/4 oz. Gran Marnier
3 oz. Sweet and Sour Mix

Directions

Fill shaker tin with ice. Add all ingredients to tin. Shake well. Sugar rim and lime garnish.

Submitted by Jeremiah Johnson's

MARGARITA'S AUTHENTIC MEXICAN FOOD

7013 N. Oak
Gladstone, MO
(816) 468-0337

2829 Southwest Blvd.
Kansas City, MO
(816) 931-4849

12200 Johnson Dr.
Shawnee, KS
(913) 631-5553

13401 Holmes
Kansas City, MO
(816) 941-9411

There are many aspects to Margarita's success. One is their philosophy that "the customer is number one." There is something to please everyone on their extensive menu. Another is old family recipes that help Chef John Abarca to dish up authentic Mexican food that melts in your mouth and keeps customers loyal and coming back. They pride themselves on using the best products and ingredients they can buy. Let's not forget where Margarita's got its name. It is named for the popular Mexican drink that contains tequila, triple sec and other ingredients. At the restaurant Margarita's are made in large batches then dispensed through a tap like draught beef. When you go to Margarita's you know you will get good service, drinks, and most importantly good food, in short it feels like coming home.

Margarita's Arroz con Leche

2 Cups Heavy Cream
1 Cup White Rice
1/8 tsp. Salt
1 Cup Sugar
1 Tbsp. Whipped Cream

1 Cups Milk
2 Sticks Cinnamon
2 Cups Half and Half
1 Tbsp. Orange Zest
1 Tbsp. Ground Cinnamon

Directions

Combine heavy cream, milk, cinnamon sticks, salt, orange zest and rice and bring it up to a boil, then down to a simmer about 30 minutes or until the rice is cooked. In a separate pan heat the half and half and add to the rice mixture and stir at a simmer. Take off the heat and add sugar and mix well. Strain and remove cinnamon sticks. Take excess milk and whip for whipped cream. Garnish with whipped cream and cinnamon.

Submitted by David and Ron

PADDY O'QUIGLEY'S PUB & GRILLE

Select Imported Irish Whiskey, Blended & Single Malt Scotch Whisky

Premium Draught Beer Selection Imported Lagers, Ales & Stout

Sláinte
(To Health)

Céad Míle Fáilte
(100,000 Welcomes)

featuring
Feasting Imbibery & Debauchery with Quenchability for All

119th & Roe, Leawood, KS • (913) 345-1119
I-470 Hwy. & Woods Chapel Rd., Lee's Summit, MO • (816) 373-5888

Paddy O'Quigley's was founded by Tom Intfen with family and friends from Atchison, KS and the Kansas City area in 1990. Quigley is the maiden name of Tom's mother's mother, the 'O' was added for a bit of flare. Other proprietors include Tom's sister Judy Intfen and Drew Mullen. The refreshing Irish approach with its warm and friendly atmosphere complements the food, which sets Paddy O'Quigley's apart from the rest. Service with a smile and a menu that's as clever as it is unique, it's the quality and quantity of food that make the difference. May the Lord and the Luck O' the Irish be always with those who visit us.

Irish Eyes

Created to help you woo your own Irish Lass.

1 oz. Lt. Rum
1 Scoop of Lime Sherbert
4 oz. Orange Juice

1 oz. Raspberry Liqueur
1 oz. Smirnoff Raspberry

Directions

Pour raspberry liqueur in the bottom of a hurricane glass. Combine all the other ingredients in a shaker with ice. Shake mixture well and pour into hurricane. Be careful not to disturb raspberry liqueur.

Irish Isle tea

1/2 oz. Irish Whiskey
1/2 oz. Vodka

1/2 oz. Rum
1/2 oz. Triple Sec

Directions

Combine ingredients in tall juice glass. Fill with sweet and sour juice and splash with coke. Shake, garnish with a lemon and serve.

Submitted by Drew Mullen

TANNER'S BAR & GRILL

12906 W. 87th St. Parkway
Lenexa, KS 66215
(913) 541-0137

The first Tanner's Bar and Grill opened in Lenexa, KS in 1985 and quickly became THE place to hang out and watch the local boys earn another victory on the big screens. You can relax in a friendly atmosphere while enjoying Tanner's famous Chicken Lips©, Boogas© or Surf-N-Turf (shrimp & steak) specials. One of the best things about Tanner's is our locations with eight locations all going strong around town and one in Lawrence, there is one near where you work and live. It's just a short drive to our great refreshments and tasty food!

"The Friendly Purveyors of Good Times, Fine Food and The Pause That Refreshes". Take Your Pause Today at a Tanner's Near You

Southern Lemonade

1 oz. Coco Ribe
1/2 oz. Creme de Noya

1 oz. Southern Comfort
Lemonade

Fill glass with ice and lemonade, coco ribe and Southern Comfort. Top off with creme de noya. Shake and serve with wedge of lemon. Enjoy!

Tail Wagger

1 oz. Smirnoff Orange Twist   1 oz. Peach Schnapps

Fill ice into 12 oz. glass. Add liquor and top it off with blend of sour mix and Sprite/7-Up.

Sun Struck

1 oz. Smirnoff Raspberry Twist   1 oz. Melon liqueur

Fill in 12 oz. glass with ice. Add your mix.

Submitted by Della Smith

Other Books From The Publisher

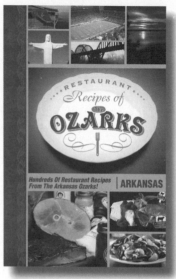

Restaurant Recipes
of the Ozarks - Arkansas

Restaurant Recipes
of the Ozarks - Missouri

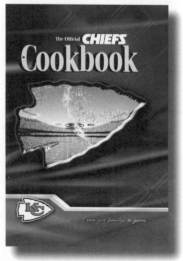

The Kansas City
Chiefs Cookbook

To Order Call:
(800) 313-5121

Index

MISCELLANEOUS

DESSERTS

BEVERAGES